CLASSIC

European

RACING MOTORCYCLES

CLASSIC
European
RACING MOTORCYCLES

Mick Walker

OSPREY
AUTOMOTIVE

Page 1
Jawa teamsters at a Czech international meeting in the mid-1960's

Page 2
Spanish multi world champion Angel Nieto (49 cc Derbi), Ulster GP 18 August 1970

Right
Barcelona 24-hour race, July 1974

Front cover
George Martinez at the 1980 Swedish GP; Martinez was 80 and 125 cc world champion on Ducados-backed machinery in the 1980s

Back cover
Ricardo Tormo at the 1961 German GP on a 50 cc Bultaco; Tormo was world champion in 1978 and 1981

Published in 1992 by Osprey Publishing
59 Grosvenor Street, London W1X 9DA

© Mick Walker 1992

Cataloguing in Publication Data is available from the British Library

ISBN 1 85532 269-2

Editor Shaun Barrington
Page design Geoffrey Wadsley

Filmset in Great Britain by
Tradespools Ltd, Frome, Somerset
Printed by BAS Printers Limited,
Over Wallop, Hampshire

Franticek Bartos (CZ) winner of the Ruppert Hollaus
Memorial Race at Salzburg, 1 May 1956

Contents

The author (left) with the legendary Derbi racing designer Francisco Tombas, November 1975; machine is a 125 cc six-speed twin from the famous Mollet, Barcelona factory

Introduction

Classic European Racing Motorcycles is the sixth and final in a series of books intended to cover the world's racing motorcycles in the fullest possible way, from 1945 to the end of the 1970s. Unlike the other volumes, which have concentrated upon a single nation, the 'Euro' volume covers eight countries; all of which although gaining a fair level of success, didn't quite justify a whole book to themselves.

The eight nations comprise Austria, Czechoslovakia, France, Holland, the Soviet Union, Spain, Sweden and Yugoslavia.

The Czechoslovakian and Spanish chapters are the two which have the most words and photographs, but the other six are in many ways no less deserving of their inclusion here.

Of course there are some European nations such as Belgium, Switzerland, or Finland who also have some claim to fame, but either their great days were pre-War (Belgium) or they produced only riders of world class, and not racing machinery (Switzerland and Finland).

A total of 14 individual marques are covered, plus various Soviet types which, although they come under a single heading, actually comprise the products of seven individual factories.

The book also encompasses a large number of talented engineers, designers and riders, many of world standing.

The FIM World Championship series was introduced in 1949 and besides the title holders from Britain and its Commonwealth, Japan, Germany, Italy and the Americas, there have been a large number of riders from other nations. These are: Austria, Ruppert Hollaus (125 cc 1954); Stefan Dörflinger (various 50 and 80 cc early 1980s); France, Patrick Pons (750 cc 1979); Holland, Jan De Vries (50 cc 1971 and 1973); Henk Van Kessell (50 cc 1974); Finland, Jarno Saarinen (250 cc 1972); Spain, Angel Nieto 13 titles in 50 and 125 cc – second highest of all time behind Italy's Giacomo Agostini; Ricardo Tormo (50 cc 1978 and 1981); Sweden, Kent Andersson (125 cc 1973 and 1974); Switzerland, Luigi Taveri (125 cc 1962, 1964 and 1966); Fritz Scheidegger (Sidecar 1965 and 1966); Rolf Billand (Sidecar 1979, 1981 and 1983). Quite some list!

Like my earlier works, I would like to record my sincere thanks to all those people who have kindly assisted me in some way with its preparation.

These include many of the factories featured; in particular KTM, CZ, Jawa, Derbi, Husqvarna and Tomos. Once again, Doug Jackson came to my rescue by providing valuable information and photographs, as did Nick Nicholls and Mick Woollett.

Other material came from Barbara Kenedi, Barry Hickmott, John Fernley, Ross Insley, the late Don Upshaw, Maurice Kelly, Davies McGuire, Terry Larner, Brian Woolley, Dan Shorey, Sammy Miller and Eric Christian.

Photographs came from a wide range of sources including Doug Jackson, Nick Nicholls, Mick Woollett, Richard Walker, the Champion Spark Plug Company, KTM, Motobecane, Monark, Husqvarna and Tomos to name but a few; plus my own collection. The cover photographs are, as always in this series, the excellent work of Don Morley.

I would also pay tribute to the efficiency of my secretary Kim White for typing the manuscript; the editorial team of Osprey, including Nick Collins and Shaun Barrington; and finally my beloved wife Susan who has always backed my motorcycling activities to the full.

It is left for me to wish you as much pleasure from reading *Classic European Racing Motorcycles* and the rest of the series, as I derived from compiling them; my intention being to provide the fullest possible coverage of the classic racing scene. I have also been lucky enough to participate as competitor, tuner, team manager, and now author over thirty years.

Mick Walker

1
Austria

Before the Great War in 1914, Austria ruled large parts of Europe. The Austro-Hungarian Empire's only real political and military rivals were Britain and France. The rivalry between these great countries was not only limited to politics and military concerns, but extended into the field of technology, where it aroused national pride. When France began organising the first speed events and long distance endurance road races, the other European nation to go along with her was Austria, who was anxious to prevent France from monopolising the glory attached to the new sport of motorcycle racing.

At the end of the 19th century, one of the classic speed events was the Paris-Vienna. Entrants to this race included specialised racing machinery from France, including the products of the Werner brothers and motorcycles that had been constructed in the Austro-Hungarian Empire by Laurin and Klement and Puch.

After defeat in the First World War, Austria was divested of some of her former territory. A result of this was that Laurin and Klement were now in Czechoslovakia (see chapter 2), and Puch was left as the only internationally-known Austrian bike builder.

Another war saw more changes; although Puch continued its dominant position, two new important names emerged after the Second World War, KTM and engine specialists Rotax, as leading marques of international repute. All three were to play an important part in the Austrian built motorcycle's revival in the 'classic' period.

KTM

KTM (Kronreif and Trunkenpolz, Mattighofen – the names of the two founders and the factory's location) produced its first machine, the 98 cc R100 in 1953.

In their early days KTM built a number of scooters and lightweight motorcycles powered by Sachs-Rotax two-stroke engines. Perhaps the most famous

and widely seen KTM production models of the 1950's were the 125 Grand Tourist motorcycle and the Pony scooter; the latter was also built under licence from KTM by the West German company, Gritzner-Kayser.

But most interesting of all the projects at the time was the superbly crafted KTM-MV Agusta 125 racer. This was basically a version of the MV Agusta single overhead camshaft Sport Competizione production racer given a double overhead camshaft top end built by the Rotax engine company on behalf of KTM. Driven by twin bevel shafts on the offside of the engine, the conversion was masterminded by the talented Austrian engineer Ludwig Apfelbáck, who had earlier designed a prototype 350 cc Horex racing twin in 1954 (see *Classic German Racing Motorcycles*, Osprey Publishing).

Other technical details of this interesting bike included an engine capacity of 123.5 cc (53 x 56 mm), a completely new (and massive) cylinder head and barrel, an all-new six speed gear cluster, with a gearchange on the left rather than the right, and a special oil tank which fitted underneath the engine and gave an improved centre of gravity. There was a choice of either telescopic or Earles type front fork assembly.

The standard single knocker MV's Dell'Orto SS1 carburettor and remote float chamber were retained, but the rear brake pedal was moved to the right to accommodate the gear lever's new position. The tachometer was driven by the exhaust camshaft. Maximum power output of the double knocker KTM-MV engine was 18 bhp at 12,000 rpm.

A team of works supported riders, including the founder's son, Eric Trunkenpolz, rode these machines to victory in several Austrian road racing championships in the late 1950's, before the company switched its efforts to dirt racers in the 1960's – a move which included a successful tie-up with the American Penton organisation. In the 1970's KTM increased this effort and was rewarded with a string

Beautifully crafted KTM-MV 125. This featured a special double overhead camshaft top end designed by *the Austrian engineer Ludwig Apfelbáck and built for KTM by the Rotax engine company*

Ing Apfelbáck at his drawing board and KTM's Hans Trunkenpolz, 1957

KTM-MV 125 racing engine. Maximum power was 18 bhp at 12,000 rpm; gearbox was a six-speeder

of world championships and ISDT gold medals, in the process becoming one of the truly great names in the history of off-road motorcycle sport.

Puch

The Puch motorcycle company has a complex history and a story somewhat reminiscent of the Swedish Husqvarna marque, starting out by being involved in armament production.

To understand why, one has to realise that Steyr-Daimler-Puch (for many years the largest private company in Austria) came about because Puch amalgamated with Austro-Daimler in 1928 and Steyr in 1934. Both Austro-Daimler and Steyr were in trouble and needed the prosperous Puch AG to survive. All these three factories had the same majority shareholder, a Vienna trust bank.

The armaments connection comes through Steyr – the oldest of the three companies. This concern was

Most sporting of the pre-war Puchs the 54, built from 1934 till 1937

founded in 1864 by Josef Werndl and he named it *Waffenfabrik Josef und Franz Werndl & Co* and its location was the town of Steyr. Already managing another firm producing armament components, it was no surprise that the new plant was built solely to make armaments. In 1869 it was renamed *Oster-reichische Waffenfabriks Gesellschaft* and quickly became the largest armaments manufacturer in Europe. By 1890 it had more than 9,000 employees turning out in excess of 540,000 rifles a year.

The year 1894 saw bicycles added to production and this sector rapidly became a major feature of the company.

The outbreak of the First World War caused rapid expansion and a production of 4,000 rifles per day was accompanied by bicycles and aero engines.

After the conflict was over, Austria was on the wrong side, with much of its former territory gone and armament manufacture banned completely. Not to be beaten, Steyr maintained its bicycle interests and also instigated car production. In 1927 the company changed its name once again, this time to the simpler Steyr Werke AG. However, the Great Depression had a devastating effect on the plant, and this prompted the 1934 amalgamation.

Austro-Daimler, the second company in the group, was originally set up in 1899 to manufacture automobiles; in fact its first task was to assemble components made in Germany at the factory *Daimler Motoren Gesellschaft* based in Weiner Neustadt. This soon led the founder Josef Eduard Bierenz to construct complete cars under licence. In 1906 the company became *Osterreichische Daimler-Motoren-Gesellschaft Bierenz, Fis & Co* and at the same time was joined by the legendary designer Ferdinand Porsche. Soon he had added buses, trucks and specialist military vehicles to the Austro-Daimler line up. Like Steyr, Austro-Daimler also put on weight during the First World War; and like their future partner, Daimler moved into cars once the conflict was over. However, the factory remained on its own only until 1928, when it linked up with the *Puch Werke AG*, to form *Austro-Daimler-Puch Werke AG*.

Now to Puch itself. Founded by Johann Puch at Graz in 1891, the original Puch enterprise was a small company manufacturing bicycles called *Johann Puch & Co*. Things went along at a steady pace with gradual improvement rather than vast expansion, the result being a well organised and profitable enterprise, but in 1897 Puch was persuaded to sell out to a German company. The terms of the sale barred him from making any bicycles for two years, but after this time he went into the two-wheel business once more. In 1899 he opened a new plant which was named *Johann Puch Erste Steirmarkische Fahirad Fabriks Aktiengesellschaft*. In 1910 he produced the first Puch car, and shortly after this the first Puch motorcycle, powered by a four-stroke single cylinder engine.

In the very early road races (up to 1905) Puch machines were fairly active, but the most successful of its racing bikes was without doubt the 1906 'Gordon Bennett'. This was a four-stroke v-twin of 904.7 cc (80 x 90 mm), with belt final drive and 3.5 bhp. These machines ridden by Nikoden and Obruba took first and second places in the 1906 European International Cup race. The make also appeared in the Isle of Man TT, but all Puch entries in the 1913 and 1914 Senior races retired.

By the outbreak of war in 1914, Puch had established itself as one of the leading motorcycle manufacturers in Europe; but that same year saw two other incidents in the Puch story. The first came on the 19th July when Johann died suddenly; the second was yet another name change, this time to *Puch Werke AG*.

Split single 125 Puch at the 1950 Dutch TT

Because it continued to build only two-wheel veh-icles, Puch was not so badly effected by the War. It was also an early convert to the two-stroke engine.

The first of the company's famous line of split-singles was the LM (Light Motorcycle) of 1923. The first successful use of this concept was the Monza, a racing 250. This was also sold in 350 cc size as the Type M. Then in 1931 came a 500 cc two-stroke with two cylinders and four pistons which turned out 14 bhp. Just to prove it was also capable of other things, in 1936 Puch designed and built a four-stroke four cylinder engine with a capacity of 800 cc.

Left
Details of 1950 125 racing Puch. Features included twin exhausts and megaphones, single downtube frame, telescopic front forks and unsprung frame

Below left
The 246 cc Puch split-single which took part in a 24 hour record bid at Montlhéry near Paris in May 1951

Below
Works 125 Puch at Hockenheim, West Germany, May 1952; note unusual design of front forks and frame. Engine is the familiar twin carb, split-single design

Puch also enjoyed a fair level of success in Euro-pean racing, including winning the 1931 German Grand Prix at the Nürburgring with a supercharged 250 split-single ridden by Swiss works rider Elvetio Toricelli, and gaining several more minor victories with the 250 cc S4 from 1934 until 1938. Puch were early users of water-cooling and supercharging. But its machines were largely overshadowed by the superior supercharged DKW two-strokes during the mid-late 1930's.

Even so Puch persevered with their split-single two-stroke concept after the Second World War, at first with a 125 cc version equipped with two carbu-rettors, one each side of the cylinder barrel. One of these was raced by future world champion Werner Haas before he was signed by NSU. Besides the machines Puch raced themselves they also supplied engine units to Dr Joseph Erhlich in Britain who used a refined version in his brave but ultimately abortive attempt to produce a competitive machine to challenge the Italian four-strokes in the early 1950's.

Before the demise of the EMC company (later to be revived purely as a racing team with machinery designed by Dr Erhlich himself), the bespectacled Hans Burman rode one of the EMC-Puchs to sixth place in the 1952 Ultra Lightweight TT at a race

average of 63.14 mph. The same rider also finished the 1954 TT on the same machine, this time in seventh place.

In the 250 cc class the Puch split-single had a limited amount of success in both racing and record breaking in the early post-Second World War period; whilst an interesting two cylinder four piston model made an appearance at Hockenheim in May 1954, but was outclassed by the latest German machines such as the twin cylinder dohc NSU Rennmax and Adler two cylinder two-stroke.

The split-single design continued in production well into the 1960s, but was not raced by Puch much after the mid-1950's, and it was not until the 1966 West German Cologne Show that the company finally got around to introducing a new breed of two-stroke.

Designated the M125, the standard production roadster single cylinder 123.5 cc (54 x 54 mm) engine produced 11 bhp at 7,000 rpm. Today, a quarter of a century later, we talk of restricting 125 cc machines to 12 bhp, but in those days this was a very good output indeed. The new bike had a five-speed gearbox and a very striking cylinder head design, with the

fins arranged in a so-called 'sunburst' pattern to promote cooling and eliminate distortion. It was an immediate winner, due largely to its sporty good looks.

To show off the potential of the new machine, Puch entered one in the 1966 ISDT. The bike had a special trials-type frame based on the 50 cc machines, but the engine was left in standard trim. The results were encouraging to say the least, the bike coming first in the 125 class and taking a magnificent second overall.

The engine certainly seemed to have some development potential and the factory once again looked at the road racing scene. In 1967, a modified M125 engine was mated to a racing chassis, making a very lightweight and elegant machine. The frame was a duplex full cradle with a fully triangulated rear section, leaving the space between the engine and the rear wheel looking completely empty. The fuel tank was very long and low and it blended well into the slender lines of the full fairing fitted on some occasions.

Hans Burman sixth finisher in the 1952 Ultra Lightweight TT on his EMC-Puch

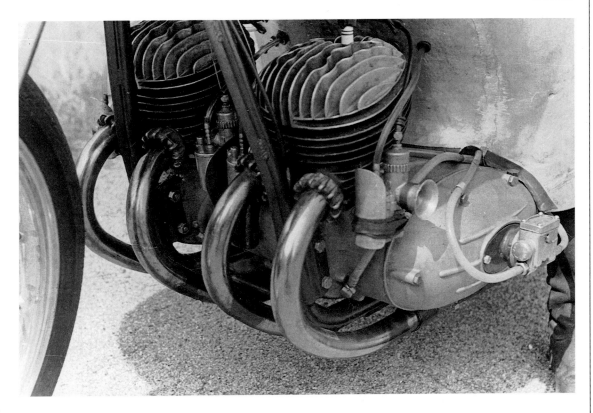

Four piston Puch twin, international Hockenheim races, 13 May 1954

A lot of development work went into the engine, especially in the area of exhaust resonance and expansion – then still a relatively new science – and into the timing of the conventional piston porting. It was said to produce 21 bhp at 10,000 rpm, and to have a maximum speed of 106 mph.

Only two of these machines were reputed to have been built, and they only made a few appearances. Interestingly, one of them ended up in Finland where it was raced under the Tunturi name. This was for purely commercial reasons, for Tunturi, who manufactured mopeds, used Puch engines in their machines. Their name can be seen today on every successful line of exercise bicycles and gymnasium equipment!

Alongside the 125 cc machines, a 250 twin cylinder racer was also developed. Effectively a doubled-up 125, the engine still had the sunburst head and twin expansion chamber exhausts. The frame was basically the same as the 125, complete with a massive twin leading shoe front brake and an equally large rear drum. It had the same slender aerodynamic fairing and slim petrol tank, making it a fine-looking machine. Power was a claimed 40 bhp at 10,000 rpm and the top speed was claimed as 124 mph. This bike also saw action under the Tunturi banner.

Neither the 125 or 250 cc machines was really successful; they did compete at the Austrian Grand Prix in 1967 in both classes, but neither finished. In 1969 at the Yugoslavian GP Jarno Saarinen rode a 125, but only managed to finish in 19th place.

Although the racing Puchs brought little glory to the old factory, their intensive development programme led directly to a completely revamped range of sports bikes. However, because of the general world-wide depression of the motorcycle industry at the end of the 1960's, Puch, perhaps wisely, put most of their efforts into the production of mopeds, including the world famous Maxi, and left the glory to the off-road machines with which they went on to win the world championship with their 250 cc moto-cross machine in the mid-1970's.

Overleaf
Interesting three cylinder 174 cc Puch special, May 1965. This homebrewed machine featured three Dell'Orto carbs, three sets of ignition coils and a three-into-one exhaust system

Above left
Puch built this neat 125 cc single cylinder two-stroke
based on their roadster engine during early 1967

Left
Technical details included piston port induction,
radial cylinder head, 21 bhp at 10,000 rpm, six speeds
and a maximum speed of 106 mph

Above
A 250 twin also made its debut in 1967, the engine
owed much to the single; later it was raced by the
Finnish Puch agents Tunturi

Top
Puch 250 twin pumped out almost 40 bhp and was
good for 125 mph; but although an attractive machine
it wasn't competitive on a Grand Prix level

Above
This watercooled 250 cc Puch twin appeared in 1978.
The engine used several Yamaha TZ components,
including the crankcases and crackshaft assembly.
Cycle parts were of Austrian design including
cantilever frame

Rotax

Like KTM, Rotax began life after the Second World
War. Initially the company built German Sachs
engines under licence, but during the 1960's they
began their own separate design work.

It was also in the late 1960's that Rotax began taking an interest in road racing. A 125 was built based
on the company's production engine; entered in
Austrian national races its good results encouraged
the Gunskirchen company to begin racing abroad.
The best Rotax rider was Heinz Krinwanek, who finished fifth in the 1969 125 cc world championship
series after a third in West Germany, a second in East
Germany and, finally, a fifth place in the last round
at Opatija, Yugoslavia.

Perhaps the most glamorous Rotax was the water-
cooled 500 cc twin which was used in both solos and
sidecars during the mid-1970's. By then the company was called Bombardier-Rotax GmbH. This had
come about after a tie-up with the Canadian Bombardier factory, who also made Can-Am motorcycles.

(Former BSA motocross star Jeff Smith was a leading
figure in this company.)

Essentially, Rotax made engines for Can-Am as
well as the Bombardier snowmobile engine. And it
was these 496.7 cc twin cylinder units which were
modified by Rotax for road racing – initially four
being lent to solo riders and two to sidecar men. The
engines, which first appeared at the Austrian GP in
May 1973, were parallel twins with inclined cylinders and modifications included water-cooling and a
special primary drive designed to mate with a Nor-
ton-type gearbox. Bore and stroke was 72 x 61 mm
and the engine revved to 9,500 rpm in solo tune, giving a claimed 90 bhp. The sidecar unit had a broader
spread of power, revving to 9,000 and producing 85
bhp.

*This interesting 496.7 cc Rotax racing twin made its
debut at the Austrian GP, 6 May 1973. The engine
was actually based on the Canadian Bombardier
snowmobile unit*

Several companies used the competitive 250 Rotax inline disc valve twin during the late 1970s and early 1980s. One such concern was the English Cotton marque; a Cotton motorcycle is shown here at the British Grand Prix at Silverstone in 1980 ridden by Graeme McGregor, who finished in 7th spot in the 250 cc race

Less impressively, the converted snowmobile engine did not prove a success in its new role, and was soon withdrawn.

Later in the decade the company built a brand-new inline water-cooled twin with rotary valve induction, which challenged the production TZ250 Yamaha in the early 1980's. Several frame manufacturers used this engine unit. In Britain these included Cotton and Waddon.

Today Rotax build a large variety of engines in both two- and four-stroke form from 125 cc upwards. The best known are the four valve four-stroke single in either 500 or 600 cc engine sizes and the 250 cc two-stroke twin so successfully used in the Italian Aprilia machines; both production and works racers. These Rotax-powered machines remain the only effective challenge to the Japanese in the hotly contested quarter-litre class.

2
Czechoslovakia

Together with Britain, France, Belgium and Italy, Czechoslovakia was one of the true pioneers of road racing at international level. The Laurin and Klement concern, founded whilst Czechoslovakia was still part of the Austro-Hungarian Empire, was a serious threat to the likes of the Paris-based Werner brothers and the Belgian Minerva company at the turn of the century.

In 1905, Laurin and Klement produced their most famous racer-a 691 cc twin cylinder v-twin two-stroke. And it was one of these machines, ridden by the Austrian Wondrick, which had the honour of winning the first truly international motorcycle race that same year, averaging 55 mph for the 170 mile course.

Subsequently Laurin and Klement were absorbed into the much larger Skoda automobile company and for several years there was a lack of both motorcycle producers and racing within the country. Between 1920 and 1940, however, a large two wheel industry emerged in Czechoslovakia, with around fifty companies at its peak, though many of these only produced simple, small capacity two-strokes. There were a handful of international class marques – Jawa, Oger, Walter and CZ- and it was to be two of these, Jawa and CZ, who would play a vital role in the European racing scene during the post-Second World War period.

CZ

CZ didn't commence motorcycle production until the year 1932, even though the company, *Ceska Zbroiovka*, was formed in 1918 to manufacture armaments. And it was Walter, rather than CZ, which really got the company into racing – which goes some way to explaining why the post-war CZ racing story involves exclusively four-strokes, rather than the 'strokers which the company used for both its standard production roadsters and the vast majority of its various moto-cross and endurance bikes.

In 1938 Jaroslav Walter, one of the two sons of the founder of the Walter marque, created an extremely modern 248 cc pushrod road racing engine and in 1939 an overhead cam version, which after the war scored a string of racing successes. In 1947 a new 348 cc ohc racing single was added, which (together with the original 248 cc version) was taken on board by CZ when Jaroslav Walter joined the much larger Stakonice factory the following year.

The period 1951–53 had seen the larger engine win several races in Austria, although it didn't have the power or road-holding of the latest Featherbed 350 Manx Nortons. An example was displayed at the Vienna Show in March 1954.

But 1955 was to be the year when CZ truly entered the international scene, with brand new bikes in the 125 and 250 cc categories and a team of three riders: Bartos (team leader), Parus and Kostir. The new team made its debut at the Swedish GP, gaining a brilliant second place in the 125 cc race. The 125 produced 14.5 bhp, the 250 24 bhp.

Both machines used dohc, unit construction engines, with five speeds and wet sump lubrication. In addition, the two designs shared the same full cradle duplex frame. But whereas the 125 used telescopic front forks, the 250 featured one of leading link design with external hydraulic dampers. Full-width alloy brake hubs were used, with a larger diameter front unit on the 250. Nineteen-inch steel rims with racing tyres completed the specifications. The 125 engine was of a much neater design than the 250, in that, on the latter, the gearbox sprocket was exposed.

The following year saw the team show up for the Austrian Grand Prix in early May, with Bartos taking victory in the 250 race. The first classic race counting towards the 1956 World Championship series was the Isle of Man TT. There were three CZ entries, the first for 21 years from a Czech manufacturer, in the shape of two for Bartos (125 and 250)

Far left
A 350 cc Walter-engined CZ four-stroke single on display at the Vienna Show in March 1954

Below far left
One of the newly designed dohc, unit construction, five-speed 125 cc CZ racers at the Austrian GP in May 1956

Left
Nearside view of double knocker 1956 125 CZ single cylinder engine. Note the neat construction and forward mounted magneto

Below
Unlike the smaller machine, the 1956 250 CZ rear had leading link front forks. Note exposed gearbox sprocket

Isle of Man 1956 250 CZ single (above) with . . .   . . . and without streamlining (below)

and Parus on a 125. All three CZs were fully stream-lined, with alloy dustbin fairings and large capacity hand-beaten alloy fuel tanks.

In the 125 race Parus finished sixth averaging 59.82 mph for the nine laps of the Clypse circuit. Bartos, though, failed to complete one lap in the race. He made amends for this by coming home fifth in the 250 event (again nine laps), at an average speed of 63.28 mph. The team went to the Dutch TT at Assen, where Kostir scored his first classic points by finishing sixth in the 250; Bartos was also sixth in the 125 cc race.

The IoM TT celebrated its Golden Jubilee in 1957 and CZ sent a team of four riders – Bartos, Parus, Kostir and Franta Stastny (later to win fame for his exploits on the 350 Jawa twin). They had two entries in the 125 race in Bartos and Parus. But in the event only Bartos took part, finishing a creditable seventh, with only the rapid works MV Agustas and FB Mondials in front of him.

In the 250 event Bartos did even better, coming home fourth in a race won by Cecil Sandford (World Champion that year) on a Mondial and in front of Sammy Miller's Mondial and Dave Chadwick's MV. Kostir came seventh and Stastny twelfth, enabling the three Czech riders to take the club team prize. As for the Continental GP's, the highlight was in Bel-

1956 IoM Lightweight (250 cc) TT practice, CZ teamster Frantisek Bartos (18) leads MV Agusta star Carlo Ubbiali

gium, where Bartos again proved his worth by finishing fourth in the 125 and fifth in the 250.

For 1958, Ulsterman Sammy Miller was signed to race the Czech single cylinder twin-cam machines. Miller's first outing was scheduled to be the Austrian Grand Prix on May 1. Following the Austrian, Sammy would fly to Britain to compete in the Scottish Six Days Trial on his factory Ariel. Although CZ had competed in the TT for the previous couple of years this would be the first time since Jawa rider/designer George Patchett's days that a Czech factory had been represented there by a British rider.

In Austria, Sammy Miller's first outing was definitely a success. Riding what was described as a 'hack' machine fitted with an experimental six-speed gear cluster (only five had been employed previously), he finished second behind World Champion Carlo Ubbiali (MV).

The motor itself followed normal CZ road-racing lines with bevel-driven double overhead camshafts, but it was reported that a new engine with twin-plug ignition would be ready for the TT. The Ultra Lightweight and the Lightweight TTs were once again

held over the shorter Clypse circuit. In the 125 race Miller rode as part of the works Ducati team on 125 Desmo singles, finishing fourth.

Motor Cycling, in its Second TT Number, dated 12 June 1958, headlined the 250 TT: The 'Race of Duels'. With three TT's to be run that day, Wednesday 4 June, the 150 Lightweight got underway early at 10am. It was a warm morning, with very little wind around the 10.79 mile Clypse course.

As the machines assembled it was clear that the race would be full of interest with a wide array of bikes: ten NSUs and an Adler from Germany; from Italy four MVs, two Guzzis, a Ducati and a Mondial; from Czechoslovakia Miller's CZ (no Czech riders were present that year), and a number of private

owner British irons. The original entry of 30 was now down to 25 due to non-starters, which included all the East Germany works MZs. According to their best times in practice, riders lined up on the grid for their massed start.

On the front row were Germany's Dieter Falk (Adler), England's Dave Chadwick (203 MV), Italy's Carlo Ubbiali and Tarquinio Provini (MVs) and Sammy Miller's six-speed CZ double knocker single.

Throughout the race Miller had a private battle with Falk's water-cooled Adler twin, which the German eventually won, thanks to the CZ rider dropping the plot at Ballacoar on the second lap, breaking the windscreen in the process. At the end of the ten-lap, 107.9 mile race, Miller finished sixth in a time of 1 hour 29 mins 8 seconds, at an average speed of 72.63 mph, with Provini taking victory from his team mate Ubbiali. Mike 'the bike' Hailwood, participating in his first race on the circuit at the tender

Left
Bartos on his way to a creditable seventh in the 1957 TT on his works 125 CZ

Below left
The Irishman Sammy Miller was signed for the 1958 season; here the CZ rider is in action on his 248 cc single, finishing sixth at 72.63 mph on the 10.69 mile lap Clypse Circuit

Below
More than 150,000 spectators attended the international races held near Tallinn, Estonia in May 1963. The winner of the 125 cc event was the CZ works rider Stanislav Malina

age of 19, finished third on an NSU Sportmax.

Next in the classic calendar came the Dutch TT. Racing started with the 250 cc class, but Miller's CZ refused to fire on the startline, leaving the Irishman at his pit to remove his helmet after a vain effort to get his machine underway.

The following weekend there was no 250 class at the Belgian GP and by the time of the next Grand Prix, the German at the Nürburgring, Miller had decided to quit his dual life as a road-racer and mud-plugger, to concentrate on the trials scene.

With their top rider out, CZ decided to confine their road racing efforts to within the Czech borders for the remainder of 1958 and the whole of 1959, and the Stakonice factory concentrated on the design of a new generation of lighter, more compact machinery both in the 125 and 250 classes.

Before this, during the summer of 1958, some of the CZ moto-cross team used a version of the Walter designed double knocker road racing engine in moto-cross events including the *Coupe d'Europe* (European Championship). However, after indifferent results the moto-cross men reverted (and stayed with) two-stroke power.

The first the western world saw of the new breed of CZ road racers came in 1960, when the Czech team made their annual appearance once more at the Aus-

The 1963 125 cc double overhead camshaft CZ single cylinder engine; note drive to cams, first by shaft to the exhaust side, then by a shorter shaft to the inlet

Machine without tank, seat or fairing. This shot provides a good view of the basic layout; note

hydraulic steering damper and large fabricated scoop for front stopper

trian GP, in early May. There were a pair of 250s – still dohc, but of much neater appearance – with one of the two having seven speeds. Even so, neither got in the first six at Salzburg. But a brand-new 125, with six speeds, ridden by Frantisek Bartos finished an impressive second in the eighth-litre class, which was won by MZ's team leader, Ernst Degner. Third was Jim Redman, on a Ducati.

Development of the new bikes continued apace during the remainder of 1960, with the Czechs not venturing beyond the Iron Curtain again until the 1961 West German GP at Hockenheim, where Stanislov Malina came home tenth. Although no CZs appeared at the 1961 TT, a 125 ridden by Malina held an impressive fourth place in the Dutch TT at Assen, until forced out near the end whilst holding fourth spot with, of all things, a broken exhaust pipe.

In 1962 CZ, with Malina, was back in the Isle of Man and finished seventh in the 125 race won by Honda's Luigi Taveri at 89.88 mph. In the Dutch TT, Malina improved on his IoM showing by scoring sixth.

The following year saw the pace quicken (at least in the appearance stakes) with Malina coming home fifth in the 125 and fourth in the 250 class at the season opener in Austria (which was still not yet a championship event). His position in the 250 class was noteworthy because for the first time a CZ single had beaten a Honda four with the West German Gunter Beer, finishing behind Malina in fifth spot on his ex-works 1962 bike, for which he had reputedly paid a small fortune.

At the end of May, Malina scored his first world championship points of the season, with a fifth at the West German GP at Hockenheim. Added to that was a tenth in the 250 race.

Although there were two riders entered on CZs at the 1963 TT (Malina, in the 125 and 250, Stastny the 250 only), neither finished a race. However, at the East German GP at Sachsenring Malina came in sixth in the 250 class and fifth and sixth in the Italian 250 and 125.

This was the year of the titanic David-and-Goliath struggle between Jim Redman's Honda four and Tarquinio Provini's fantastic Moto Morini single, only decided at the final round at Suzuka, Japan, with the advantage going to Redman. The following year, 1964, was to prove the Czech company's most successful yet on the tarmac.

Works rider Malina getting a helping hand to start his new 125 CZ twin for the pre-race warm-up at the 1964 Isle of Man TT

The 1965 125 CZ twin – if only the Czech company could have had this bike five years earlier . . .

Once again their international season started at the Austrian GP, which was fast becoming a good pointer to form for several classic teams. The 1964 event was held in warm, mainly sunny weather. The course consisted of two mile-long sections of the Munich-Vienna autobahn, linked by cobbled approach roads.

After a fourth in the 125 race, Malina gave CZ its first international road race victory by winning the 250 event. Having shot into an early lead, Honda teamster Bruce Beale was soon passed by both Malina and Bertie Schneider on a works Suzuki square four. Then the Suzuki rider went ahead of the CZ single, but the Czech machine was really flying; when Scheider slowed after putting up the fastest lap, Malina pulled past into the lead. The Czech finished with an easier than expected victory when, two laps from home, the infamous square four went onto three cylinders to limp home fourth.

Then came the Isle of Man TT and more success, with a pair of fourth places – and it was that man Malina both times. In the 250, his fourth place and bronze replica could have been even better had it not been for some cruel luck on the last lap. After snatching third place from Provini's ailing Benelli-four, the end of the fifth lap had seen Malina behind leader Redman (Honda) and Shepherd (MZ). But there was drama on the sixth and final circuit. Malina was forced to stop at Union Mills, 'to make adjustments' as the commentator put it, before rejoining the race. These adjustments, which allowed Pagani on the Italian Paton twin to gain third place in the final results,

were a collapsing rear wheel (broken spokes, in fact). Forced to take things steady for almost a whole lap there was nothing the Czech could do to retrieve the situation. Even so Malina's race average was a highly respectable 85.51 mph.

In contrast, Malina's brand-new 125 twin ran faultlessly to average 85.16 mph, almost as fast as his 250 time, to finish fourth again – this time behind the Honda trio of Taveri, Redman and Bryans. In fact the CZ rider was the only non-Honda in the first eight. As *Motor Cycling* put it: 'Now we can hear a really crisp engine note – it's Stanislov Malina on the high revving little CZ twin'.

The 125 twin was an extremely lightweight machine at 75 kg (165 lbs). This helped some way towards compensating for its lack of sheer power compared with its Japanese rivals. Its 124.6 cc twin-cylinder engine, with each short stroke 45 mm cylinder bore and 39.2 mm stroke, used dohc, with bevel gear distribution. With 24 bhp, maximum power was generated at around 14,000 rpm, almost an identical figure to the works Honda RC145 of 1962 both in power output and engine revolutions. However, by the time CZ brought out their twin, the Japanese company already had on their drawing boards the four cylinder RC146 which could turn an extra 10 mph at least, compared to the Czech bike's 115 mph.

Prior to the TT, the CZ 125 had made its race

Above
Maximum speed of the tiny Czech 125 twin was over
115 mph with the dolphin fairing fitted

Below
Sturdy duplex frame with twin top rails of the 1965
124.6 cc CZ twin

Above
Frantisek Bocek with the 293 cc CZ dohc single at the 1965 Austrian GP at the Salzburg autobahn course

Right
The well known Czech 'Frankie' Stastny with the smaller 246 cc version of CZ's double camshaft single during the 1965 Lightweight TT; he finished fifth. Photograph was taken at Ramsey Hairpin

debut during April at an international meeting in Modena, Italy; but except for its fine showing in the Isle of Man, the new twin found the competition just too tough. Even mighty Honda didn't have it all their own way with Suzuki hounding their every move and Yamaha and MZ in the picture too.

Later in the year a larger version of the 246 cc dohc single appeared. Again ridden by Malina, the new 293 cc (75 x 69 mm) engine finished third in the 350 Italian GP behind Redman and Beale on Hondas and in front of Pasolini (Aermacchi), Duff (AJS) and Ahearn (Norton).

In 1965 came the news that the Austrian Rudi Thalhammer had purchased an ex-works 250 CZ single. The debut for this new combination was the 1965 Austrian GP, where Thalhammer came home third behind Stastny on another CZ single, with the race going to an MZ twin. But before this, in late April, had come the first classic of the new season, the West German at the Nürburgring. In the 125 race the CZ twins came in ninth and tenth, piloted by Havel and Bocek respectively.

Although no CZs appeared in the Isle of Man, the team competed in several GPs that year, gaining the following results to add to those already mentioned: Dutch TT, Stastny fifth, 250 class; East German GP,

Stastny fourth, 250; Czech GP, Bocek sixth, 125 and Stastny sixth 250; Italian GP, Stastny fifth 250.

Around this time it should be remembered that the bulk of the CZ factory's efforts were going into the moto-cross field, with Joel Robert snatching the world title in 1964 and Victor Arbekov retaining it for the Czech concern in 1965.

During 1966, Bocek and Stastny were the official riders. The days of Jawa/CZ had now firmly arrived and although the bike was a CZ, the programme said Jawa; and of course Stastny continued to ride a *proper* Jawa twin in the 350 class. Just to confuse the issue further, Stastny also rode in the 500 class that year on a machine referred to as a Jawa/CZ. This was in fact a bored out 350 Jawa dohc twin. The CZ highlight that year was Bocek's fifth place in the 350 TT

on his 293 cc single, averaging 92.45 mph in a race won by Agostini (MV).

The next development came in the winter of 1966/67. The decision was taken to retire the obsolete 125 twin and 250 single and concentrate on the 350 category.

With their 293 cc overbored 250 proving reasonably competitive, the CZ race shop reasoned that an even bigger version with an improved power-to-weight ratio would prove worthwhile. After the revamping it emerged as a 347 cc, with a bore and stroke of 80 x 69 mm, compression ratio of 11:1 and twin spark ignition.

With detailed internal improvements, power was increased to 45 bhp at 9,600 rpm – 4 bhp more than the best AJS 7R or Manx Norton. At 105 kg (232 lbs), weight was about 27 kg (60 lbs) lighter giving the Czech bike a definite advantage. Main external alteration was the use of a clutch mounted on the engine mainshaft and running in oil. The gearbox retained six ratios.

The riders of the full 350 single were Bohumil Stasa and Karel Bojer, but their best position in the 1967 classics was Stasa's sixth at the Czech GP. For

Bohumil Stasa with a full 350 (actually 347 cc) version of the long running single; note unusual twin exhaust pipes on the same side. Hutchinson 100, Brands Hatch, England, 10 August 1969

1968 the faithful single was once again increased in capacity, this time to 372 cc, allowing it to compete in 500 cc events. Stasa finished fifth in its debut at the West German GP at Nürburgring. The 350 raced by both Stasa and Bojer took victory in the Austrian GP, fourth in the Dutch TT and another fourth at the Italian at Monza, where Stasa had only the multi-cylinder MV and Benellis in front – soundly beating Bruno Spaggiari's factory Ducati Desmo single and Stastny's Jawa twin.

Next year started off with yet another victory by Stasa on the 350 single in Austria. But none of the various entries from Bojer or Stasa finished a race in the Isle of Man. There were also several minor leaderboard places at Hockenheim, Sachsenring, Imola and Opatija. But the real sensation, if only from a technical viewpoint, came at the home Czech round in the world series.

At Brno, team leader Stasa appeared in practice

with a revolutionary four cylinder machine. In the race though, he came sixth on one of the old singles. It had been back in 1967 when the two engineers responsible for the CZ road racing effort, Ing Frantisek Pudil and Ing Josef Brejcha, decided to create something *really* different. This was to emerge as a V-four, with dohc valve operation. The air-cooled engine had each pair of cylinders banked at 90 degrees, the top two cylinders being 10 degrees from vertical (inclined backwards), with the lower pair of cylinders facing forward.

With a capacity of 346 cc (50 x 44 mm), the engine was constructed oversquare, not only to allow for higher revs, but in addition to provide the best layout for the combustion chamber shape. Continuing this line of thought came four valves per cylinder and a single 10 mm sparking plug per pot. The West German Mahle forged pistons were provided with only two (against the conventional three of a normal four-stroke) piston rings in a somewhat speculative

Right
CZ star Bohumil Stasa; he rode the dohc singles of various capacities and the innovative v-four

Below
Another Stasa shot, this time on an overbored 372 cc CZ single at the Ulster Grand Prix, 16 August 1969

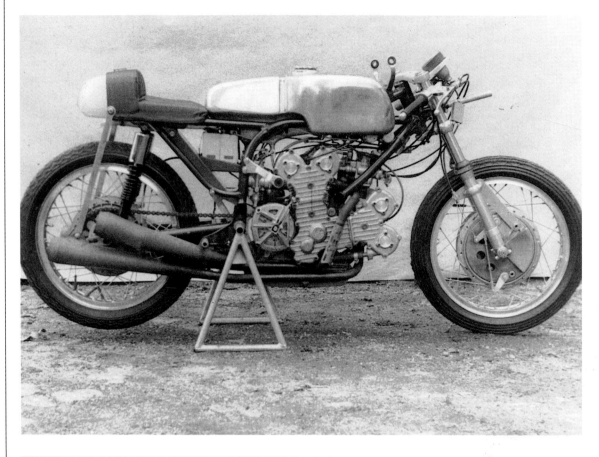

Above
The CZ v-four which first appeared at the end of the 1960s. It was designed jointly by Ing Frantisek Pudil and Ing Josef Brejcha

Left
The first prototype 346 cc (50 x 44 mm) v-four made its debut in 1969

Above right
Air-cooled dohc v-four engine had each pair of cylinders banked at 90 degrees

Right
The engine formed a stressed member of the frame

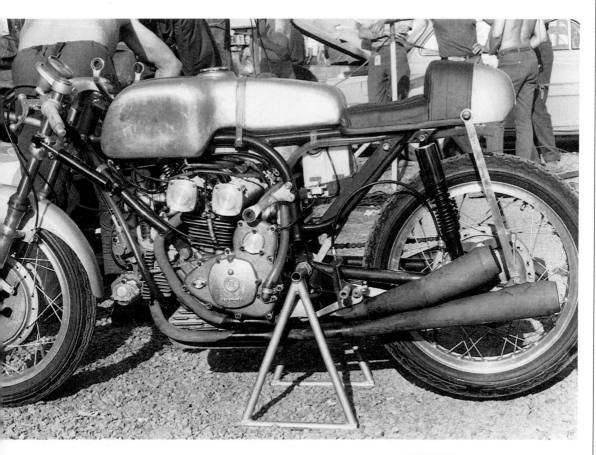

attempt to keep friction to a bare minimum.

The design of the crankshaft was of particular interest. The con-rods for both left- and right-hand cylinders were disposed to the big-end next to each other on one crankpin. The crankshaft was supported at three points within the crankcase assembly, but both the cage of the middle bearing and the inner ring were divided. The reason behind this was that in order to ensure the necessary higher rigidity in the centre section of the crankshaft, it meant that particular attention had to be taken in machining the crankshaft. This special central bearing was made at the National Czech Research Bearing Institute in Brno. Lubrication for both engine and gearbox was provided by castor oil contained in the large finned sump at the base of the crankcase.

The gearbox was an eight-speeder. Each cylinder was provided with its own 25 mm Dell'Orto SSI racing carb with remote float, each pair of cylinders sharing a single fuel chamber.

Ignition was simple in the extreme, with twin batteries/coils and twin contact breakers. The points themselves were mounted on the end of the crankshafts of the top cylinders on the nearside. The designers would have used a different set-up had it been available to them, such as an electronic system. Primary drive was by helical gear with a multi-plate dry clutch mounted on the offside.

The frame, to an original design, used the engine crankcases as an integral stress member in a similar way to that used on the Ducati V-twin of the 1970s. Much of the balance of the machine was of Italian origin, including the Ceriani forks and brakes, a 230 mm Ceriani front and 200 mm Oldani rear.

The initial power output of 52 bhp at 13,000 rpm just couldn't match the other multis of the era. In 1969 the MV Agusta 350 three cylinder offered 63 bhp and the Jawa four cylinder two-stroke which Bill Ivy rode that year pumped out 70 bhp. But following more work that winter the CZ engineers managed to up this figure to 58 bhp, which at least gave it a chance of competing with the best privately-owned Yamahas, but not the MV or Jawa. Without a doubt the four cylinder CZ's finest hour came in the 1971 Czech GP, when Stasa finished as runner-up to the Flying Finn Jarno Saarinen on his works Yamaha.

The final development of the four (and for that matter the CZ four-stroke racing saga) came late in 1971, with the machine emerging as a full 500. In this form it at last proved a race-winner when Stasa won

CZ works rider Stasa with the 350 CZ four during practice for the Austrian GP, 25 April 1970

the 750 race at Jicin, Czechoslovakia in July 1972. At this demanding circuit, the Czech V-four beat Kawasaki rider Charlie Dobson by 12 seconds and hoisted the outright lap record to 94.35 mph.

This all came too late however, as the factory had already officially retired from road racing at the beginning of 1972 to concentrate its efforts on meeting the ever increasing demand for its utility roadsters from Eastern bloc countries. Its only sporting involvement from then on would be off-road. This was a sad end to a machine which if given more priority in its early life could well have provided a viable challenge on the Grand Prix scene in the late 1960s. As it was, this design concept, albeit in a different form, was taken up by the Japanese years later to achieve the success which Ing Pudil and his small team of enthusiasts had known about when designing their V-four – that of a narrow engine with less height, offering penetration at high speed.

With their singles, twins and fours, CZ provided

Czech GP 1971, 350 cc race: Stasa CZ four (7) amongst a pack of riders including the Hungarian Szabo Yamaha TR 2B (12) and Duba CZ Single (29)

race enthusiasts with an alternative marque for almost two decades, even though their efforts were never more than a few outings per season. Today, sadly, their efforts have all but been forgotten.

Jawa

The Jawa story begins back in 1929, when with the country almost totally reliant upon imports to satisfy its craving for powered two-wheel transport, Ing Frantisek Janecek, of the National Arms Factory in Prague, decided his company should become involved with motorcycles. He obtained a licence from the German Wanderer concern to build one of their designs – a 498 cc ohv single, with unit construction and shaft drive. Other features included a pressed steel frame and leaf-spring front forks. Although the Czech-built bike did not sell in any real numbers and proved troublesome in service, it did coin a new name in motorcycling: Jawa (from the first two letters of the names Janecek and Wanderer).

The next move came when leading British designer George Patchett joined Jawa in 1930. It was Patchett who put the new company on the map with a string of successful designs, including a racing

machine with a 500 ohv unit construction engine, four speeds and chain final drive. The racer was later redesigned with a separate gearbox. Patchett, who was also a rider of some note, produced a 348 cc model, and later still competitive mounts with 173 and 248 cc engines.

In 1932 Jawa introduce their first two-stroke, a modern looking lightweight with a 173 cc British Villiers deflector piston engine. A succession of roadsters followed with two-stroke and side valve power units. Apart from the Villiers and Wanderer engines made under licence agreements, all were the work of George Patchett. But with the onset of War in 1939, Patchett returned to England.

During the conflict Jawa, at their Tynec and Prage-Nusle factories, repaired motorcycles for the occupying German forces. Even so, they managed to prepare for the post-War period by designing and developing a new range of motorcycles. One of these was an ultra-modern 248 cc two-stroke single, with unit construction, automatic clutch (which was to remain a feature of Jawa roadsters for many years), telescopic front forks and plunger rear suspension.

In 1947 Jawa swallowed up the rival Oger factory and introduced a brand-new model, a 346 cc two-stroke twin which employed many cycle parts from the 248 cc single. It was also during this period that the first post-War racers appeared. Created by a new designer, Vaclav Sklenar, these were 348 and 498 cc dohc, vertical twin engines in supercharged and unsupercharged forms. Riders included Dusil, Novotny, Rykr, Stainer and Vitvar.

Jawa had been nationalised at the end of the War and a link was formed with old rivals CZ in 1949 when both companies came under the control of the Czech Auto Industry. With the post-War boom in motorcycle sales, Jawa were able to finance the development of yet more racers. Designed by Jozif and Krivka these too were dohc parallel twins, with capacities of 248, 348 and 498 cc.

Initially, the twins were only seen within the Communist bloc but in its push for exports the factory sent its works team to do battle with Norton, Moto Guzzi and BMW on the Continental circus. In July, 1954 Jan Kostir appeared at Zandvoort in Holland and promptly won the 500 race from noted British and Dutch privateers.

Reported at the time to have been developed from a standard production 488 cc single overhead cam parallel twin roadster, the racer was really substantially different. With a capacity of 498 cc, it had a bore and stroke of 65.75 x 73.6 mm, power output was claimed to be 45 bhp at 7,000 rpm, giving a

Englishman George Patchett played a vital role as designer and rider during the early days; he's seen here at the Isle of Man TT in 1932

maximum speed of 128 mph.

The duplex cradle frame was manufactured in square section tubing. Front suspension was a heavy hydraulically-damped telescopic fork, with full swinging arm rear design. Interestingly, both wheel rims were of 16 inch diameter. This gave the bike a squat, even tubby, appearance. Tyre sections were 3.00 and 3.25 ins respectively. The brakes featured alloy full-width hubs of 250 mm (10 ins) diameter, with lining width of 36 mm ($1\frac{3}{8}$ ins), front and rear.

The crankcases were unusually tall and constructed in elektron. The four-piece, built-up crankshaft was carried in a single row ball race on the timing side, with a double row bearing on the drive side. Steel connecting rods with single row roller bearing big-ends were employed. The forged, three-ring pistons had slightly domed crowns and cutaways to clear the valves. Both the cylinder barrels and heads were in light alloy; combustion chambers were hemispherical. Each of the overhead camshafts was supported by three roller bearings, and driven through a vertical shaft and two sets of bevel gears from the offside of the crankshaft.

Lubrication was of the dry sump variety and

transmission by means of a duplex chain to a four speed, cross-over-drive gearbox in unit with the engine. The ignition was by a Bosch magneto mounted atop the crankcases at the rear of the cylinder barrels. Two 30 mm carbs were connected to their manifolds through rubber pipes, each of which were $3\frac{1}{2}$ ins long. Exhaust gases ran out into large diameter straight-through pipes which extended aft to the rear wheel spindle line.

Although the 498 cc twin continued to be raced successfully at home and abroad, Jawa did not make its post-War classic debut until the Dutch TT at Assen in June 1956. Here Gustav Havel came home twelfth, on a 350 version. The 350 had made its debut, outside the 'Iron Curtain' at the Swedish GP in July 1955, ridden by Havel and Franta Stastny.

Over the winter a new 248 cc vertical twin was built. With bore and stroke of 55 x 52 mm the design closely resembled the NSU Rennmax with its camshaft drive details and primary drive with three gears. Producing 30 bhp and revving to 11,000 rpm, the engine was carried in a duplex frame, with telescopic forks and swinging arm rear suspension.

The quarter-litre engine was to form the basis of Jawa's GP success in the late 1950s and throughout most of the next decade.

Stastny set the ball rolling with fifth place at the

July 1954, the 500 Jawa dohc parallel twin with which Jan Kostir appeared at Zandvoort, Holland and promptly won first time out from noted British and Dutch riders

Dutch TT of 1957, bringing his dustbin-faired bike home behind a trio of Mondials and an MV, but it was not until 1960 that the Czech factory began to shine. By then the 250 had become a 350 and a considerable re-design had taken place.

Although it was still a unit construction dohc parallel twin, the vertical shaft had now been moved *between* the cylinders at the rear and drove the inlet camshaft by means of bevels. A horizontal shaft, lying along the top of the engine took the drive forward to the exhaust camshaft.

Double helical valve springs were featured. Each cylinder barrel and head was a separate casting in light alloy. Steel liners were employed for the cylinder bores. The engine had a bore and stroke of 59 x 63.5 mm. The oil was now carried in a deeply-finned wet sump, in place of a separate oil tank.

A pair of double-ended ignition coils supplied the sparks to the two 10 mm plugs in each cylinder head. A distributor was mounted on the offside of the crankshaft. A pair of spur gears on the nearside unit took the drive from the crankshaft through a multi-

The Jawa 500 parallel twin, as it appeared in 1956, with . . .

. . . and without its streamlining

plate clutch to a six speed gearbox. A feature of the design was that the gearbox could be removed without dismantling the remainder of the engine. Measured at the gearbox output shaft, peak engine power was 46 bhp at 10,600 rpm.

An all-welded duplex frame had its main portion constructed from 28 mm ($1\frac{1}{8}$ ins) diameter tubing. The twin loops were brought closer together behind the power unit and passed inside the bearings in the swinging arm pivot instead of outside, which was the more conventional arrangement. A pair of adjustable Girling racing springs and hydraulic units looked after the rear suspension, whilst fibreglass was used for the fuel tank and rear mudguard. Rims were 19 ins, laced to full width 210 mm twin leading shoe, cable operated drum brakes. Avon racing tyres of 3.00 and 3.50 section were specified.

A simple quick-release method of attaching the dolphin type fibre-glass fairing was used. On the end of the tubular mounting stays were cones which located on thimble-shaped metal sleeves, moulded into the inner face of the fairing which was retained by rubber bands. Such detail was typical of the thought given to maintenance in the design. Dry weight was 120 kg (265 lbs), similar to the latest version of the 250 twin which produced 36 bhp at 10,800 rpm.

At the first of the 1960 classics, the 350 French GP at Clermond Ferrand, Stastny sensationally split the MVs of Hocking and Surtees to finish second. And at the last GP – the Italian at Monza – Stastny again finished second behind Hocking, this time with Hartle's Norton taking third.

Across the Atlantic, the United States' 250 national records for 3–400 miles at 1–6 hours in flying and standing start categories were smashed by a production 250 Jawa Street Scrambler at Daytona International Speedway with speeds between 74 and 77 mph.

In 1961 Jawa's fortunes began to see-saw. Stastny led the 350 race in a non-championship Salzburgring meeting until forced to retire with clutch trouble after five laps. The same problem put him out of the 250 event. His team mate, Havel, who took sixth berth in the quarter-litre scrap, followed Stastny

Right
Czech challenger, at the Salzburg races, 1 May 1956

Below
250 Jawa twin, the forerunner of the successful 350 version which followed the next year; Franta Stastny is the rider

Original 350 Jawa looked like this, circa 1960

into the 350 lead but crashed, fortunately without injury, two laps from the finish.

All this was forgotten a week later when the Czech pair took the one-two in the 350 – Jawa's first ever Grand Prix victory since the world championship series was initiated in 1949. Over the Hockenheim circuit much had been expected of McIntyre and Brambilla with their Bianchi twins but both soon retired, and with no MV in the race, Stastny and team-mate Havel forged well ahead of the field and only four riders remained unlapped at the end of the 20 lap, 96 mile race, won at an average speed of 112.42 mph. Stastny's fastest lap was 113.98 mph, (compared to Hocking's race winning MV in the 500 category of 124.86 mph).

Following this came the Isle of Man TT where Stastny finished fifth in the 350 behind race winner Phil Read's Norton, Hocking's MV and Ralph Renson and Derek Minter (both on Nortons). Havel finished way down the field in 27th position on his Island debut.

Next date on the 1961 calendar was the Dutch TT, where once again Stastny put in an excellent performance, finishing third behind Hocking and Bob

McIntyre's Bianchi and in front of Brambilla on a similar model.

Back in Czechoslovakia, the Jawa team had a field day at a rain-soaked Jicin, respectively second and third to Jim Redman's Honda four in the 250 race. Stastny and Havel were first and second in the 500 race on 350s. The 350 race went to the Russian rider Cada, on another Jawa, from Perris and Findlay (Nortons).

At the end of July came East Europe's first post-War classic. Some 250,000 spectators saw Stastny finish second behind Hocking's MV and in front of Bob McIntyre's Bianchi. Havel was fourth on the second Jawa at the East German Grand Prix at the Sachsenring. There were several Jawas present, and two of them were fitted with what looked like oil tanks under the saddle. In fact this container was simply a tank to collect oil mist.

The 1961 East German GP was also one of the very last outings for the 250 twin, three of which competed. Havel was the only finisher, gaining only ninth place. Phil Irving, writing for *Motor Cycling* at the time, commented: 'This whole machine is too big and heavy to have much chance of success.'

Strangely, it was also at Sachsenring that a rumour started that the Czech company might give up road racing. The press reckoned that, as the factory had only one small shop to handle its race, trials and moto-cross mounts, it was operating at a severe disadvantage. Its racers were all dohc four-strokes whereas normally production was confined to two-strokes. As events were to prove, the rumours didn't have much substance. Jawa went on to score second and third places in the 350 world championship that year.

After East Germany came the Ulster, where Stastny finished third, a position repeated at Monza by Havel when Stastny was forced to retire. The final classic of the 1961 season, the Swedish GP at Kristianstad, saw Jawa repeat the 1–2 of earlier in the season, when Stastny won from Havel.

After the excellent results in 1961, the following year was an anti-climax. Stastny's second place in the Ulster was the highest placing. This was due in no small part to more competition in the 350 class. Not only did Jawa, MV and Bianchi continue, but they were joined by Honda and even a brand-new four cylinder Soviet racer, the S360, which made its debut in East Germany. All this was reflected in the end-of-season league table which saw Redman and Robb finish first and second, Hailwood third on an MV and Stastny fourth in front of Bianchi new boy Grassetti.

Considerable development went on inside the Jawa's engine for 1963. The biggest change was that of four valves per cylinder. The high-domed forged three-ring pistons featured small squish areas at the front and rear of the piston crown. And the lighter weight of individual valve assemblies enabled the factory to push up peak power revs from 10,600 rpm (for the 1962 two-valve model) to 11,400 rpm for the four valver. Meanwhile maximum power was boosted $1\frac{1}{2}$ bhp to 52 bhp. To minimise camshaft bending in the four valve layout, there was a roller bearing between each pair of cams. Besides central plugs and squish piston crowns to match, the other change for the four valve layout was split ports. An unsuccessful modification was that of twin plug ignition – the twins were subsequently raced for the rest of the season with the second plug of each cylinder blanked off.

Without doubt the highlight of that year was Stastny's third place in the IoM TT, where the Czech brought his uprated twin home behind race winner Redman's Honda and Hartle's Gilera. It was the team's highest GP placing that year for the Jawa team leader crashed at Jicin after the engine seized. His right leg was broken in eight places and Stastny missed half the season. Even so, he repeated his

Stastny with part of his trophy collection, March 1961 – lots more were to come

Stastny's side-kick in the Jawa race team of the early 1960s, Gustav Havel; although he never won a Grand Prix, Havel provided reliable back-up

fourth place in the 350 world championship.

Pavel Slavicek was then brought in to back up Gustav Havel, Slavicek proving his worth by finishing fifth at Monza. By now their design was being rapidly outpaced but Jawa engineers continued to develop the dohc twin. During the closed season of 1963/64 several more improvements were introduced. Most obvious was the new duplex front brake and new side panelling – the latter claimed to keep water out of the carburettors. Internally, the crankshaft and crankcase were strengthened to withstand the higher revs permitted by the change to four valves per cylinder. Finally the crankshaft could now be withdrawn from the crankcase much more easily without disturbing the gearbox.

Early in 1964 also saw the first signs that Jawa were considering a switch to two-strokes, with a story in the 16 April issue of *Motor Cycle* proclaiming: 'Jawa are to race a four cylinder five-hundred!' This exciting news, which came from Czechoslovakia, said that the machine might be ready for the TT, but certainly would be completed for the Dutch and Belgian classics.

Engine was said to be a two-stroke square four with rotary inlet valves. A single carburettor, bolted to the side of the crankcase, fed each pair of cylinders. *Motor Cycle* also went on to say: 'Brainchild of a Jawa factory mechanic, the project was enthusiastically received by the firm who foresaw tremendous

1961 Isle of Man Junior TT, Franta Stastny at Ginger Hall on the 350 Jawa twin; he finished fifth in the race and second overall that year in the world championship series

possibilities in the design when developed.'

First of the 1964 classics was the Isle of Man. Here seven 350 Jawa twins arrived for Stastny (still limping heavily from his Czech tumble the previous year) and Havel. After holding second, on the fourth lap Stastny was forced out with faulty rear suspension. Near the end of the race, well down the field, Havel spilled at Windy Corner, luckily without injury.

In the Isle of Man Stastny had chosen to ride a model with two valve heads and a 180 degree crank while Havel rode one of latest four valvers.

The team fared no better at the Dutch TT, so the first two classics had passed without a single point being scored. Then came the West German GP, around the 11.45 kms Solitude circuit near Stuttgart. In practice Stastny crashed on some oil and broke the same leg in six places, snapping the metal plate inserted after his previous crash. Stastny, now 37 years old, was out for another long period. Even so, Havel, after scoring a second at Sachsenring and a third at Dundrod, was still able to finish fifth in the championship series.

If 1964 had been disappointing for Jawa, 1965 was to prove just the reverse – both from a results point

Franta Stastny leads Tommy Robinson (AJS) at the annual international Finnish Elaintarha meeting, 13 May 1962

of view and technically. The factory Jawas were out for the first time on Italy's Adriatic coast for the Cervia race in early April. The biggest change to the 350 twin was a new, lower duplex frame clearly modelled on the 125 CZ twin design. Features included eccentric adjustment of the rear wheel and a specially strengthened steering head layout. Interestingly, the two valve engines were used – influenced by a spate of big-end failures with the higher revving four valve layout the previous year.

At the classic season opener at the Nürburgring, an experimental 250 two-stroke twin made its debut. This had disc valves and closely resembled the earlier air-cooled MZ. The engine, with a bore and stroke of 54 x 54 mm peaked at 12,000 rpm and had a six-speed box. There was also talk of fitting one of the Russian four cylinder engines into the new lower 350 Jawa frame.

Stastny missed the first few meetings recovering from his accident, and it was not until the wet 350 East German GP that he scored his first points when he made up the meat in a Jawa sandwich, with third, fourth and fifth places going to the Czech team on revamped twins.

Meanwhile development of the two-stroke twin continued, with prototype 125 and 350 versions built. At the same time it was generally believed that the long-running dohc twins would be phased out by the end of the year. But a surprise was just around the corner and it happened in Northern Ireland.

As the August 12 issue of *Motor Cycle* summed it up: 'Expect two things from the Ulster Grand Prix – rain and surprises. Both were closely linked last Saturday at Dundrod, near Belfast.' With the opening 350 cc race sewn up, Jim Redman (Honda) crashed on a rain-sodden road on the last lap and presented veteran Czech, Franta Stastny (Jawa) with a surprise win. Redman collected a broken collar bone.

Fired with fresh enthusiasm after this Ulster GP victory, Jawa decided to construct an overbored version for use in the Italian GP at Monza the following month. Initially reported to be a 420 cc, it turned out to be only 352 cc, and fifth in the 500 race

Above
Gustav Havel in action during the 1964 Ulster GP.
He finished third with only Jim Redman (Honda) and
Mike Duff (Yamaha) in front

Ulster Grand Prix 8 August 1964. Left to right: *Bert*
Schneider (Suzuki works rider), Malcolm Edgar
(Castrol 'trade baron') and Jawa teamster
Gustav Havel

gave Jawa their first championship points in the class.

Influenced by the advent of the Yamaha fours and six cylinder Hondas, Jawa concentrated development on the new two-stroke twin 350. But as the 1966 season began their only truly raceworthy bikes were the faithful 350 and the larger version – now finally increased to 420 cc. And, indeed, it was the larger class which proved the most rewarding, with Stastny gaining another GP victory (in East Germany) and finishing third in Holland and Ulster. He finished fourth in the 500 world championships and, despite his highest placing being second, he also finished fourth in the 350 series.

Excellent results these were, but the decision had already been taken to finally pension off the four-stroke twins. Their replacement, the 350 air-cooled two-stroke twin was not to prove the answer. Used for the first time in Czech GP practice, its performance was disappointing. But worse was to follow. Practising for the Italian GP, Stastny was lucky to escape injury when the engine seized at high speed, throwing him down the road.

It was decided to concentrate on the disc valve 500

Above left
New lower frame for the 1965 season and double
sided front stopper for the now ageing 350 dohc twin

Left
Jawa tried twin spark ignition and four valves per
cylinder in an attempt to remain competitive with
their four-stroke twin

Above
The first ever Jawa production racer was a 247cc two-
stroke single based around the 'flying banana'
motocrosser. It went on sale in 1967

Right
A batch of singles awaiting delivery at the factory in
early 1967; performance was on a par with British
singles such as the Greeves Silverstone

four-cylinder described earlier. Now water-cooled and with the cylinders in vee formation, the first official hint came in September 1966 that a 350 version was also on the cards. The engines were reported as having two crankshafts geared together and six-speed gearboxes.

After all this, it is extraordinary that in January 1967, fresh news came out of Czechoslovakia of several more new and revised projects. First a 250 Jawa production racer. This used the 'flying banana moto-crosser as a base. The single cylinder 246 cc (70 x 64 mm) featured conventional piston port induction and with a 12:1 compression ratio and 32 mm Jikov carb offered 31 bhp at 7,250 rpm and a top speed of 116 mph. This put the bike on par with British production racers such as the Greeves Silverstone. A batch of twenty bikes was initially built.

But far more exciting was news of a new 125 class

Above
Technically interesting 125 two-stroke narrow angle v-twin helped Jawa gain experience, in 1967

Below
Clutch and primary drive details of the experimental v-twin

two-stroke v-twin; a new 250 two-stroke parallel twin; a 350 twin with more power; and by mid season the 350 version of the four cylinder V-four. Quite some programme!

By April, first concrete information was to hand on the all-new 125 two-stroke V-twin. The air-cooled unit was carried horizontally beneath the frame with the two crankshafts geared together to drive a seven speed gearbox. The gearbox was technically unusual. In reality it had been designed as a four speeder, but a supplementary two speed 'overdrive' unit – adopted to keep the box narrow – gave a theoretical choice of eight ratios. However, this was considered excessive, and to provide the correct steps between the ratios the number of speeds was reduced to seven.

The tiny 124 cc Czech V-twin consisted of two 44 x 41 mm bore and stroke air-cooled cylinders positioned on a common crankcase, set at 18 degrees to each other. Each cylinder had its own separate crankshaft with disc valve induction. And as each crankcase ran its own pressure-sealed compartment within the common crankcase each of the cylinders were in effect two separate 62 cc engines. These breathed through a pair of 24 mm Amal GP carbs and ignition was by coil and battery with twin contact breakers positioned alongside the clutch. The pressed-up crankshaft assemblies were supported by needle roller bearings on the drive side and by ball bearing which also located the assembly axially, on the other side. Both the big- and small-ends were caged roller bearings.

To ease maintenance problems the engine was designed so that the crankshaft assemblies could be removed individually without taking the engine out of the frame. The cylinders were light alloy, longitudinally finned, with pressed-in steel liners. There were three transfer ports and one exhaust port, but all four were bridged to give a total of eight per cylinder. Forged pistons were fitted with an orthodox single hard chromed ring. The pistons featured large ports cut in their skirts to mate up with the third transfer port.

In bench tests the individual cylinders could be run separately by removing the splined driving gear from the crankshaft of the unwanted crank assembly. This allowed identical power curves to be plotted for the cylinders to make sure that when they were running together as a normal engine, both were giving full power. In tests, the power output of each single 62 cc cylinder was around 14.5 bhp at 14,000 rpm – an output of some 230 horse power per litre. Running as a unit the best figures were 27 bhp.

The frame was a duplex assembly made of chrome molybdenum tubing, with the engine suspended from three mountings. British Girling suspension units controlled the movements of the bronze bushed swinging arm. A multi-plate dry clutch was fitted, mounted externally to assist both cooling and maintenance. The sintered friction material was bonded onto the plates. Front forks had 32 mm stanchions and 180 mm twin leading shoe, full width, drum bakes were used front and rear.

The fuel tank was made in fibre-glass and extended down close to the top cylinder to deflect cooling air onto the cylinder as well as to get the centre of gravity as low as possible.

Two of these highly interesting lightweights were made – and their real purpose was not to contest races but to provide the basic information to help in the development of other higher capacity multicylinder two-strokes.

Early in the year Stastny was in the wars yet again when he broke a thigh whilst racing one of the new single cylinder production machines. And this meant that 1967 was deemed as a development year, rather than a serious race year in the Jawa camp. The new 350 V-four two-stroke made its race debut at the Dutch TT in June. Finished only a week earlier, it seized three times in practice and had a final seizure while being raced by Havel.

The engine followed the vee layout of the Yamaha fours – though it had in fact been thought up entirely independently. The two crankshafts were geared together – and used much of the technology used on the 125 V-twin. Induction was again by disc valve, which designer Zdenek Tichy thought absolutely necessary for ultimate performance (as did MZ and Yamaha). The 344.5 cc (48 x 47.6 mm) engine had a compression ratio of 16:1 and usable power between 9,000 and 13,500 rpm. Drive to the rear wheel was by a chain, via a seven speed gearbox.

Unlike the Yamaha, water-cooling was on the thermosyphon principle, and it was generally accepted that the appearance of the Czech unit was a lot tidier than the Japanese fours, although in 1967 it was not in the same speed category.

On the prototype engine there were four sets of contact breakers and the four Amal GP carbs each had their own, flexibly mounted, float chamber.

Stastny, now back in the saddle, tested an example of a 250 V-four that summer at Prague airport. He was claimed to have clocked 145 mph. This machine was very similar to the 350, but used Dell'Orto carbs.

Three weeks after the Dutch TT though, Jawa

*The initial version of the infamous 350 v-four
appeared in late 1967; Jawa were to give it the
designation R67*

turned up at the East German GP with the old four-stroke 350 twins! The new four, first used in Holland, was under further development back at the factory in an effort to overcome main bearing failures and piston seizures.

A pump was now used in the water cooling system and tests were being carried out to see if fitting an oil pump would assist engine lubrication.

Except for a fourth by Havel, 1967 proved very much a year for experiments, rather than results. Quite simply the new 'strokers were in need of a lengthy development period and were not yet up to the rigours of long GP-type events.

It was much the same in 1968 and it was mid-

Above
350 cc v-four power unit showing water-cooled cylinders and separate carbs

Above right
Side view with carburettors removed. Disc valves, tacho drive pick-up and gearbox sprocket are all evident in this previously unpublished photograph

Right
Chassis details of Jawa's 350 v-four; although comprehensive it was pushed to cope with all the power which the motor was capable of producing on full song

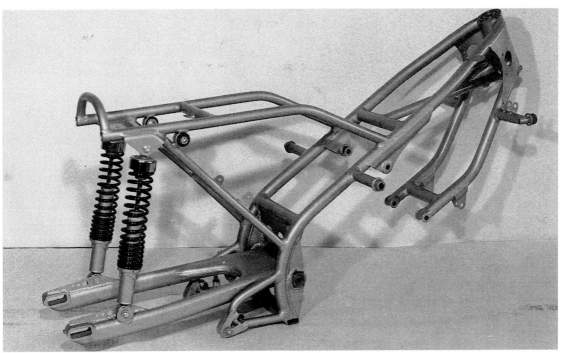

Above
After Bill Ivy was killed in 1969 several riders were given a race test on the v-four. One of them was the former Bultaco works star New Zealander Ginger Molloy, shown here with the machine at the Czech GP, 19 July 1970

Right
Another was the Italian Silvio Grassetti. He is shown here winning the Yugoslav Grand Prix, 14 September 1969, Jawa's first GP victory with the design

season before the V-four 350 first finished a classic. This was appropriately at the home round at Brno, where Stastny, now back in race condition, brought one of the two-tier four cylinder two-strokes home third – despite being hampered by cramp. Stastny's average speed was 85.65 mph, compared to race winner Agostini's MV 88.86 mph. He followed this up with a fourth at the Ulster GP and a sixth at Monza's Italian GP.

On the surface it appeared that at long last the new breed of Jawa GP racer was getting its act together. Certainly it was fast (around 160 mph) but Stastny admitted to being none too sure of its reliability and it was still prone to seizures.

At the end of the season Yamaha announced their

retirement from Grand Prix racing. One of their two top riders, Bill Ivy, thought that the Jawa could present a challenge to MV – he changed his mind about retiring from two wheels and joined the Czech team instead.

With his great experience of racing multi cylinder two-strokes for Yamaha, Ivy seemed the ideal man for the job. Ivy's debut on the Jawa four came at Ces-

Left
Jawa produced a completely new 250 single cylinder racer in 1969. Unlike the earlier dirt bike-based machine, this one was a purpose-built road racer with water-cooled engine and full duplex frame

Below left
Works rider Franta Stastny aboard one of the singles during the Belgian GP, 6 July 1969. He came home 16th, a lap behind the winner

Below
This air-cooled 250 Jawa twin had limited success in 1971/72 with Czech riders Bohumil Stasa (formerly with CZ) and Frantisek Snra, but couldn't seriously challenge Yamaha in the classics

enatico, Italy on Sunday 13 April, 1969. But it was not to be a happy outing, and after clocking the seventh best practice lap, the Czech two-stroke misfired badly in the race and seized on lap ten.

Before Ivy had signed Jawa had already ruled out the opening Spanish GP and the Isle of Man on cost grounds. So it was at Hockenheim and the West German GP that Ivy had his first classic outing with his new team.

Although the race was won by Agostini and MV, Ivy was not far behind and had given the Italian his closest battle for some time. To cap this, team mate Stastny on a second machine was third.

The third round was the IoM, but then came the Dutch TT at Assen. Here Ivy showed his mastery with a brilliant ride when, after a poor start, he caught and passed the world champion before the Jawa slowed, allowing Agostini to sneak victory.

By now, at last fitted with electronic ignition, the engine was producing 70 bhp at 13,000 rpm giving it a performance equal to that of the previously uncatchable MV three. So as the GP circus moved behind the Iron Curtain to compete in the East German event at Sachsenring, many observers thought it possible that Ivy and the Jawa four could beat Ago

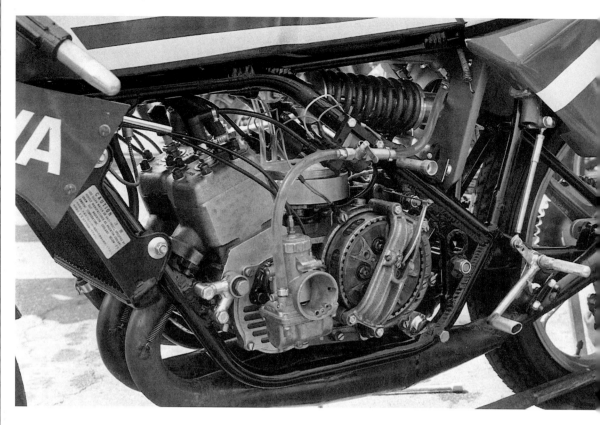

Above
The final Jawa racing engine in 1977, the water-cooled, disc valve, six speed twin – this one has a British Maxton frame

Below
Englishman Eddie Roberts race tested the machine in 1977, but Jawa were not eventually to make a Grand Prix comeback

and MV. Sadly it was not to be, a crash during practice cost Bill Ivy his life – and effectively ended dreams of glory for the Czech factory.

The cause of the accident was discovered when the 350 four cylinder Jawa engine was stripped by race officials a few hours afterwards. They found that the crankshaft of the engine's lower left hand cylinder had seized. This had occurred just as Ivy shut off for a 90 mph left hand curve entering the town of Hohenstein-Erstthal during a wet morning practice session. Bike and rider had slid along the road for a considerable distance before striking a low concrete fence which had not been protected by straw bales. Ivy's helmet appeared to come off before the impact.

He was rushed to the hospital with head injuries. Three doctors fought to resuscitate him with a heart massager, but their efforts were in vain. And so on 12 July 1969 Britain lost a true champion and the Jawa racing effort effectively died with the little man from Maidstone.

Hidden amongst the great grief and shock of the tragedy was that Bill had been due to compete in the 500 cc class of the GP on an enlarged version with a capacity of just over 351 cc.

After Ivy's fatal accident, the flames of passion for road racing at the Jawa factory effectively died. Some of this can be traced to that other great Jawa rider Franta Stastny who, now almost 40 years old, didn't want to ride the fast but temperamental four and ended his racing days on a private Yamaha TR2 in 1971.

With its potential as the only serious challenger to the might of MV Agusta, other riders were attracted to the fearsome V-four. Amongst these were Aussie Jack Findlay, the Italian Silvio Grassetti and New Zealander Ginger Molloy.

Grassetti was the most successful, finishing second in the 1969 Italian GP behind Phil Read and his private Yamaha twin and then winning the last round in Yugoslavia – but in that race second place went to Gilberto Milani on a single cylinder Aermacchi, as all the other multis had either retired or not been entered.

When he rode the Jawa in 1970 Grassetti was unable to capture his form of the previous season. And although it was raced occasionally over the next two years the 350 V-four never again repeated its performances of 1969.

The last piece of the Jawa racing jigsaw came in the 250 class. With a rehash of the air-cooled 250 two-stroke used experimentally in 1967, the factory had limited success in 1971/72 with Czech riders Bohumil Stasa and Frantisek Snra, but couldn't seriously challenge Yamaha.

After this, for a couple of years, Jawa abandoned the field, and most pundits thought that this was the end of Jawa's racing career. But in late 1976 a totally revised machine was introduced. This had a displacement of 246.3 cc (56 x 50 mm) with rotary disc induction, water-cooling, produced 44 bhp at 12,000 rpm, and had a six speed box.

At last it seemed as if Jawa might be able to challenge for honours, but all this was to come to nothing, even though an example was race-tested in England by Northerner Eddie Roberts during 1977.

So, for the last decade and a half the name Jawa has not been seen in a Grand Prix race programme – and at the present time seems unlikely to. But this doesn't hide the fact that for some twenty years the factory enjoyed a chequered career on the race circuits of Europe and during that time achieved a level of success unknown to any other marque from the then communist bloc.

3
France

It may come as a shock to many, but France was the first country to organise and promote road racing and also the first to initiate widespread motorcycle production.

Well before the end of the nineteenth century several separate French-based individuals had created organisations to explore the use of the yet untried Otto-cycle engine and thus create a fledgling motorcycle industry.

These early pioneers included Count de Dion; his mechanic Georges Bouton; Maurice Fournier, Felix Theodore Millet and Ernest Michaux. In addition, the Russian-born brothers Eugene and Michel Werner had settled in France and become Frenchmen through adoption. All these men had a hand in placing France at the very forefront of innovation as the twentieth century began.

Much of the original technical development concerning automobile, aviation and motorcycling interests was carried out by the French. But strangely, although they built up a considerable automobile and aviation presence in world markets in the following decades, French motorcycling didn't benefit in the same way. In fact only Peugeot and Motobecane were destined to grow into large concerns, and they both largely restricted their efforts to the home market.

On the racing front, once Peugeot departed the scene in the early 1920's the next truly significant French racing effort was to be a full fifty years in the future, when Motobecane introduced a new 125 twin cylinder two-stroke in the early 1970's. A similar situation existed amongst the French in the riding department – leaders in the pioneer days and then a half century break before the likes of Patrick Pons and Marcel Rougerie appeared on the scene in the 1970's.

Motobecane

Together with Peugeot, Motobecane dominated the French motorcycle scene for over sixty years. Founded in 1923 by Abel Bardin and Charles Benoit in an old electric motor factory in Saint Quentin, their first two-wheeler was a 175 cc motorcycle with belt drive. The success of this machine – it sold in excess of 100,000 units – was to prove decisive in the company rapidly establishing itself as France's premier manufacturer to a point where in the early 1970's it could claim to be the world's largest producer of mopeds and bicycles.

By this time the Motobecane empire was vast, an industrial corporation with three main companies, Motobecane, Motoconfort and Polymecanique. Motoconfort started life in 1925, two years after Motobecane but only existed as a separate company for some five years before being swallowed up. While the other member of the trio started in 1928 in order to build motors for the first of the group's motor-assisted cycles; twelve months later it went into mass production with a 98 cc engine which clipped onto the standard Motobecane pedal cycle frame.

During this period in the 1920s Motobecane also acted as an assembler for various other manufacturers including English Blackburne and French Zuchers with side and overhead valve engines of 250, 350 and 500 cc. This was a clever move because it kept the production facilities fully occupied. Because of this, Motobecane was far less affected than other manufacturers when the economic

Above left
Water-cooled Motobecane 125 disc valve twin as it appeared at Silverstone for the British Grand Prix, August 1977

Left
Works rider Thiry Espie during the 125 cc British GP, 6 August 1978. He finished 4th in the race and 5th overall in the world championship series that year

disaster struck worldwide in the late 1920s.

After this came 500 cc and 750 cc air-cooled ohc and ohv four cylinder models with shaft drive. These proved popular mainly because of their extremely competitive pricing. Co-founder Charles Benoit, who was also the firm's chief designer, came up with an entirely original 98 cc four-stroke for the 1937 season. This was the start of the very popular Z range. The first model was soon followed by larger 125 and 175 versions and these were so well received that they remained in production for almost a quarter of a century until 1963. Even then it was only the introduction of driving licences in France for machines above 125 cc which finally killed off the range leader. And in any case, by then motorcycles were going out of fashion as the buying public switched to the small family car in their droves. The drastic fall in motorcycle sales came at exactly the same time as a disastrous period for Motobecane's scooter, so bad in fact, that the small wheeled machine conceived in the mid-fifties to combat Lambretta and Vespa was finally pensioned off.

The reader can rightly ask the question, how did the marque survive? Their salvation was the humble moped, which, since the late 1930s had been a prominent feature of their production. Whilst the rest of the French motorcycle industry went to the wall, Motobecane simply switched its production. The Motobecane moped can be traced back to late 1938 when the Pony 60 was introduced. Without doubt this would have achieved even greater sales had not its early life been so savagely interrupted by the outbreak of War the next year.

After hostilities came to an end, the company was soon back in the picture and a revised version, the Pony 50, made its entrance in 1946 with its engine capacity reduced from 59 cc to 49 cc. On 30 November 1949, one of the most important dates in Motobecane's history, the first real Mobylette mopeds came off the Saint Quentin production line. As if to prove the soundness of the original design, the basic Mobylette was to remain unchanged for over 30 years.

Engines for the mopeds were manufactured by Polymecanique in their Patin factory and were then built up into the pressed steel frame back in Saint Quentin in their various specifications. The two

Espie's machine with the cosmetics removed

important features of the Mobylette range were its reliability and excellent finish. In 1965 the Cady model appeared, claimed to be the lightest moped in the world, and then in 1967 a small wheeled version was launched, the Cady II.

As the sixties came to an end, and with the introduction of machines like the Honda CB750 four and Kawasaki Mach 3, France like other European countries began to witness a rebirth in demand for larger capacity motorcycles. Anticipating this boom, Motobecane once again began the design of full-scale motorcycles – a 125 twin and a 350 triple, both two-strokes and in line with Japanese technology. Before this, they had built the Sport 50 which used a five-speed version of the old moped engine, later versions even featured indicators and a front disc!

The 1972 Paris Show was chosen to launch the

Right
Motobecane rider Guy Bertin won several GPs in 1980 and missed the championship by a mere nine points after 10 rounds

Below
Bertin in action during the 1980 Dutch TT

new 125 twin and this sported every modern convenience, including electronic ignition. Also shown in prototype form was the 350 triple, plus the unique fold-away Moby Xl. Utilising the 49 cc power unit, the Xl was equipped with small diameter alloy wheels, folding handlebars and a special telescopic seat mounting. This allowed the tiny bike to be folded away and put in the boot of a car. Although the Moby X1 was not the success that the company had hoped, its successor, the Moby X7, was a sell-out.

Motorcycle racing made a dramatic revival in France during the early 1970s, when French riders like Leon, Pons, Rougerie and Bourgeois made international names for themselves. Basking in their return to the limelight, the French began to take a renewed interest in the sport. This was one of the major reasons why Motobecane decided to develop a racing version of their newly introduced 125 twin cylinder two-stroke.

The original idea was to offer a 'training' machine for up-and-coming riders before progression to a pure grand prix mount such as Yamaha, Aermacchi or Bultaco.

Called the *Cliente* (customer) the Motobecane racer was introduced in 1973. It was powered by an air-cooled parallel twin piston port two-stroke with a capacity of 124.88 cc (43 x 43 mm). The individual inclined cylinders were cast in aluminium alloy with cast iron liners. Primary drive was by helical cut gears, and there was a five-speed close ratio gearbox in unit with the engine.

This first effort was good for around 110 mph and produced 26 bhp at 13,000 rpm. The Cliente proved itself a reliable if not super swift performer. Several privateers carried out their own tuning with the result that the bike won a number of minor races at home and just over the border in northern Spain during its first year.

In March 1974 Motobecane announced that it was to make an official return after some 40 years out of the sport, with a pair of works twin-cylinder machines. But the fuel crisis, coupled with a shortage of special metals they were to use for the engines, meant that the effort was cut to a single machine.

The rider chosen was Eric Offenstadt and it was hoped that together with a pukka racing version of

Previous page
The 1980 Motobecane GP bike; the horizontal arrangement of the 124 cc rotary valve water-cooled twin ensured a low centre of gravity and provided superb handling

the new 350 triple, a crack could be made for world championship honours in 1975.

In May 1974 Offenstadt debuted a new water-cooled engine which was reputed to produce around 30 bhp. Weight with streamlining was only 68 kg (154 lb). The bike also sported cast alloy wheels, disc brakes front and rear, and lightweight Italian Marzocchi front forks. The full duplex frame was of Motobecane manufacture.

Offenstadt and the works twin put up some good performances in French national racing, but at world level against the likes of Yamaha, Derbi, Malanca and Maico the French duo were totally outclassed.

Meanwhile the air-cooled 'over-the-counter' racer continued to notch up wins and places in minor events; whilst Motobecane experienced a terrific rise in demand for their standard production machines – which effectively meant bread-and-butter mopeds. By the mid 1970's everywhere one went in France, however remote the area, you would always see one of the company's mopeds – they were as popular as any small car and much cheaper to run.

Sadly all this was not to last. Not only did sales tail off dramatically as the 1970's came to a close, but the company also experienced several costly failures – like a range of up-to-the-minute trail bikes which failed to win any real sales even though they were a match for any of the imports from Italy or Japan.

In an attempt to fight back and attract new sales, Motobecane embarked on the World Championship trail with an all new horizontal 125 twin, and but for crashing twice while leading, once in Spain and once in England at Silverstone, rider Guy Bertain would surely have been class champion in 1980. As it was, the Motobecane star missed out by a mere nine points at the end of the season. To be fair, the accidents were not entirely the rider's fault: in Spain his rear tyre was worn out and at Silverstone the engine is believed to have seized.

The horizontal arrangement of the 124 cc (44 x 41 mm) rotary valve water-cooled twin ensured a low centre of gravity and provided superb handling. The fairing took full advantage of this with the radiator mounted in the nose section. The small size of the engine allowed the main frame tubes to run in a straight line from the steering head to the swing arm pivot. The chain tension was adjusted by an eccentric at the swing arm pivot.

This 1980 bike was very much a purpose-built factory racer and owed nothing to the earlier roadster inspired over-the-counter machine. It was built in a special race shop and the gearbox, for example, was hand crafted and machined from solid aluminium.

Some of the technical details included four transfers and one exhaust port per barrel, a pressed up four-bearing crankshaft with needle rollers for both big and small ends, a forged single ring piston, straight cut primary drive gears, six-speed 'box and a pair of 29 mm Mikuni carbs. The clutch was a dry unit with 14 plates. Front and rear suspension were Marzocchi with triple Zanzani hydraulic discs operated by aluminium Brembo calipers on Campagnolo cast wheels.

Unfortunately the machine's full potential was never to be realised, as its chief designer, Jean Bidalot, left the company at the end of 1980 to work for the Pernod drinks company specifically to produce a brand new 250 GP bike. A further blow was that Guy Bertin moved to the newly formed Sanvenero team for the 1981 season.

This spelled the end of the Motobecane racing effort. It was also to prove the end of an era, as by 1982 the company was caught up in the international motorcycle recession. This time even mopeds failed to save it and in 1985, the Yamaha concern gained a

foothold in the company's affairs. Today, Yamaha own the factory completely, with small capacity Japanese-designed machines rolling off the French production lines.

Nougier

If Britain could claim special builders such as Geeson, Marsh and Jones, then France had the Nougier brothers. Like their counterparts on the other side of the English Channel, the Nougiers were nothing if not brave – their first design being a five-hundred four! First laid out on the drawing board in 1950, and making its first appearance in 1953, it followed Italian practice with the double overhead camshafts driven by gear pinions set in a case between the middle cylinders.

The Nougier brothers built many interesting specials, but their finest effort was this 496 cc dohc four. First laid out on the drawing board in 1951 it made its debut in 1953

The engine had square 54 mm bore and stroke dimensions which gave a capacity of 496 cc. Running on a compression ratio of 10.5:1 the maximum engine revolutions were 11,500. Claimed power output was in the region of 47 bhp.

Other details included four 28 mm Italian Dell'Orto carburettors, gear primary drive, a dry clutch, cast iron cylinders, alloy heads, a massive finned sump at the base of the engine with a capacity of 1.1 litres and magneto ignition. Originally there was a four-speed gearbox, but this was later changed for a five-speed cluster.

The double cradle tubular frame had swinging-arm rear suspension and originally employed Earles-type front forks of British construction (later changed to telescopic with a substantial fork brace). Tyre sizes were 3.25 ins x 19 ins front and 3.50 ins x 19 ins rear on alloy wheel rims. The large full-width light alloy brakes were of special note, being the work of the rider Paul Collignon; the front having a dimension of 210 mm.

Up to 1958 the Nougier four's outings had been restricted to hill climbs, but in the autumn of that year the top sidecar drivers Florian Camathias and Helmut Fath both called at the Nougier family home in the South of France to see if the constructors could be encouraged to develop the engine further.

Although this visit created a good deal of publicity abroad it did not seem to influence development greatly; however in the early 1960s the four, together with a 248 dohc vertical twin made several appearances in domestic competition. Coming at a time when the French motorcycle industry was at an all-time low the Nougiers and other 'special' builders gave their countrymen something to be proud of, even if the bikes were never world-beaters.

4
Holland

Unlike their near neighbours in Belgium, the Dutch could not claim much history in the way of racing motorcycle construction until after the Second World War; this even though Assen had long been a major circuit for Grand Prix events.

The exception to the above was the Eysink marque who fielded machinery both before and after the War. The post-War period saw Excel and Jamathi make up a trio of Dutch racing marques, albeit at different periods of time.

Both Eysink and Jamathi have their respective histories charted below, whereas the Excel challenge was on a much more limited scale, the 1967 Dutch GP being the company's only classic race. Here the machine, a 50 cc two-stroke coded X16, designed by Aad van Excel, was ridden by the talented Cees van Dongen, but unfortunately struck mechanical problems and was forced to retire.

The engine of the Excel was equipped with disc valve induction, rear facing exhaust port and water-cooling. The seven-speed gearbox was built in unit with the engine and gear selection was achieved by a locking bar in the output shaft.

As well as the Dutch GP the X16 made several appearances in national events in the Low Countries during the late 1960's whilst Aad van Excel was also involved with the Jamathi racing effort.

Besides the three marques mentioned above there was also the team set up by Henk Van Veen, the Dutch Kreidler importer. As outlined in the German volume, the Van Veen effort was one of the premier teams in the smallest displacement class for many years and won a host of GP victories and world championship titles.

Eysink

This company, which could trace its origins back to the beginnings of the Twentieth Century, was the one Dutch motorcycle marque which competed in tarmac racing both before and after the Second World War. In addition, AP van Hammersveld, riding as Eysink, was the only Dutchman to compete in a pre-Second World War Isle of Man TT, when he rode a Rudge-engined Eysink in the 1934 Senior TT. Following the War Eysink built a series of small capacity two-strokes powered by modified British Villiers engines.

The year 1948 saw the introduction of a 125 cc at the Dutch GP. The race attracted the likes of Nello Pagani and Rafaele Alberti from Italy (both mounted on Morinis) and four Spanish riders on Montesas. There were a further 24 entrants on assorted machinery from the host nation.

From this contest an Eysink ridden by D Renooy emerged victorious, completing the six lap (62 miles) event at an average speed of 61.28 mph, compared to second placed Pagani who managed 60.44 mph. T Heinen on another Eysink was third with a race average of 60.05 mph.

The following year, 1949, saw the introduction of an official world championship series, including the 125 cc catogory. At the Dutch round the previous year's winner, Renooy, again Eysink mounted, led from the start, but fell at Bertelds Bocht – a hairpin corner about $1\frac{1}{2}$ miles from the start. Although unhurt, the machine was too badly damaged to continue. Eysinks were placed sixth, eighth and eleventh out of twelve finishers.

From there it was downhill all the way, albeit slowly at first. As the new wave of Italian dohc four-strokes such as Mondial and MV Agusta grew in strength, so the piston-port two-strokes such as Eysink slowly slipped from the Grand Prix scene until a single finisher in eleventh spot in the 1955 Dutch GP saw Eysink disappear completely from the classic racing arena.

Right
Eysink rider D Renooy, the class winner of 1948
Dutch TT. He took just under the hour to complete the
62-mile even for 125 cc machines

Below
The 1951 version of the Villiers based 125 Eysink
two-stroke racing engine

Final version of the Eysink as it appeared in the mid-1950's. By then it sported a duplex frame, telescopic forks and swinging arm rear suspension

Jamathi

The Amsterdam-based Jamathi-Nederhorst company grew from the efforts of two men, Jan Thiel and Martin Mijwaart. Both were skilled engineers and their first 50 cc racing special made its debut in 1962 with a first GP appearance in the Dutch at Assen where the bike came home in ninth position – ridden by Mijwaart himself.

The following year a third man joined the tiny team, in the shape of leading Dutch flyweight rider, Paul Lodewijkx. Lodewijkx soon showed his worth by gaining a number of important placings in both the Netherlands and in Belgium; the highlights being a sixth place in the domestic GP, followed by the same result a week later in the Belgian GP held over the ultra-fast Spa circuit.

If anyone had thought the 1967 Jamathi was a fluke, 1968 was to rock such critics back on their heels. Lodewijkx finished the season second overall in the 50 cc world championships. And this came after contesting only three of the five rounds!

Jamathi's season started with Lodewijkx splitting a hoard of local Derbis in the Spanish round to annex fourth. Following the Isle of Man, which the Dutch team did not contest, came the real shock: 'Home-

made 50 wins Dutch TT' said the front page headline of the *Motor Cycle* in the 3 July 1968 issue.

Perhaps the most surprising event was when the Jamathi combination beat the reigning world champion Hans-Georg Anscheidt and his hi-tech works Suzuki twin.

The engine which powered the winning bike was a water-cooled version of the 1967 machine and was a single cylinder disc valve, two-stroke with a nine-speed gearbox. Completed just hours before practice started, the engines (there were two) were capable of revving to over 14,000 rpm. Almost all the engine components were of Dutch manufacture, although the water was circulated by a Suzuki pump above the gearbox and the front brake was also a Suzuki component. Even so it was a truly fantastic achievement. Other technical details of the race winning Jamathi motorcycle included a capacity of 49.6 cc (40 x 39 mm) and a maximum power output of 14 bhp at 14,000 rpm.

Lodewijkx followed up his success in Holland with a brilliant second eight days later in the Belgian GP. His Jamathi went so fast at Francorchamps that the Spanish Derbi team protested – but the Dutch had the last laugh as the engine measured exactly 49.6 cc! Lodewijkx's average speed for the five lap, 43.8 mile race was 90.08 mph; the tiny Dutch bike was touching well over 110 mph down the longest straights.

Into 1969 and Paul Lodewijkx rode the little

Left
Water-cooled Jamathi engine as it appeared at the West German GP, 21 April 1968

Above
Co-designer of the Jamathi racing machines, Jan Thiel working on one of the engines in 1969

Jamathi against the full might of Kreidler and Derbi. The German and Spanish contenders were fighting for the championship title after the Japanese companies had withdrawn from the 50 cc class. Although Lodewijkx didn't win the title, the Jamathi team did have the satisfaction of winning three GPs; Czechoslovakia, Italy and Yugoslavia.

At the end of 1969 the Dutch rider Aalt Toerson, together with team manager Johan Leferink and chief mechanic Jan Smit, quit the Van Veen line-up, hoping to join Jamathi. But Amsterdam dealer and Kreidler importer Henk Van Veen, with whom Toerson had a two year contract, vetoed the move. However a huge public outcry followed, forcing Van Veen to relent. The moment of truth came with a medical examination on Paul Lodewijkx, Jamathi's number one rider from previous years, who had sustained head injuries in a road accident during October 1969. Doctor's reports showed that Lodewijkx would not be fit enough to race for much of the forthcoming season. So, since the Dutch Jamathi team would have stood no chance against Kreidler or Derbi without either Lodewijkx or Toerson, Van Veen at last relented and gave his blessing for his ex-teamster to ride for rivals.

Jamathi in fact fielded three riders that year: Toerson, plus Mijwaart and Stripacuk. All three responded by gaining leaderboard placings.

Aalt Toerson struck a purple patch mid-season, with victories in three consecutive GPs: Belgium, East Germany and Czechoslovakia. But unfortunately for the tiny Dutch team the results either side of this were less promising and the Derbi-mounted Angel Nieto retained his championship with Toerson and Jamathi as runners-up.

That 1970 season was to prove the highpoint of the Jamathi effort with Hans Meyer only managing to finish fifth in the 1971 championship title race, whilst Theo Timmer came home third two years running in 1972 and 1973. But the talents of Jan Thiel and Martin Mijwaart were not to be wasted and the duo went on to design several other Grand Prix bikes for the likes of Piovaticci, Bultaco and Cagiva among others.

Top
Partly built Jamathi in early 1969. Most components were of Dutch manufacture; notable exceptions being the front brake and water pump, both of which were Suzuki components

Above
Start of 1969 50 cc Belgian Grand Prix. Numbers 4 (Lodewijkx) and 50 (Mijwaart) are on Jamathis

Above right
Ulster GP, 15 August 1970. Jamathi's new signing Alt Toersen (3) leads the Derbi rider Salvador Canellas. Canellas eventually finished 2nd, Toersen 3rd

Right
Aalt Toersen's 50 cc Jamathi at Dutch TT, 26 June 1971. Note lighter frame and Fontana front brake

*Jamathi rider Theo Timmer leads Jan Huberts
(Kreidler), Italian GP at Monza, 20 May 1973*

5

Soviet Union

Motorcycles were not made in any great number in the Soviet Union until 1928, when a few experimental road going models were produced in Izhevsk. Much of this was because under the Czar industrial development was frowned upon; then followed the First World War and finally the Bolshevik revolution in October 1917. All these events made it impossible for Soviet engineers to undertake the design and construction of motor vehicles alongside their European contempories.

The first Soviet machine to enter anything like series production was the M21, which went on general sale in 1930. Powered by a 300 cc single cylinder two-stroke engine which was similar to the German DKW of the period, the M21 launched the USSR onto two wheels.

There followed a period of imitation, resulting in 1931 in a bulky 350 cc four-stroke model with a Harley Davidson engine and gearbox. In 1935 something closely resembling a 595 cc BSA Sloper was introduced under the code name TIZ-AM-600. The American type machine was reflected in the PMZ-A-750. Manufactured in Podolsk to the design of the Scientific Motor Tractor Institute, this sported coil ignition with gear primary drive, a three-speed gearbox and pressed steel frame.

Although learning what they could from the West, Soviet engineers were also beginning to show the fruits of their native research.

The Kharlov factory developed a 250 cc two-stroke with an enclosed pressed steel 'shell' and just prior to the outbreak of the Second World War Podolsk was working on an original 125 cc two-stroke with integral gearbox.

During 1938 Soviet machines began to boast improvements long enjoyed elsewhere, such as twist-grips, foot-change and full electrical equipment. The advantages of the single cylinder, over-head valve four-stroke engine now began to be appreciated, although the Russian industry still largely depended upon the more basic two-stroke.

In 1940 (Germany did not declare war on the USSR until June 1941) came the Izhevsk, a machine which appeared to be an almost direct copy of the 350 cc DKW. Another face seen before with a different coat of paint was the M72, a 750 cc flat-twin four-stroke, with shaft drive, telescopic front fork and plunger rear suspension and known elsewhere as the BMW R71.

However, the quality of these Soviet 'copies' was often mediocre.

After the War large sections of the USSR lay in ruins and it was all hands to the pump to put the country back on its feet again. The idea of motorisation had also captured the hearts of the Soviet people and realising this the Communist Party and its officials responded by launching a programme to satisfy these needs.

As motorcycles were less costly to build than four-wheelers, the Soviet Union chose this path to satisfy much of its private demand for transport in the immediate post-war era. And since the Germans had lost after all, the Soviets did not think it necessary to bother about patent rights and therefore began to imitate machines such as DKW and BMW – both of which had plants in the eastern sector of Germany which was now under Soviet control.

The two main types to be mass produced were the 125 cc Moskva two-stroke – the DKW RT125 design (also copied by BSA in Britain and Harley Davidson in the USA amongst others) and the M75, the Soviet version of the flat-twin BMW. These two machines were also pressed into use as road racing machines before more specialised designs took over. Below are details of the Soviet-DKW racing story, the BMW one follows similar lines.

At the termination of hostilities in 1945, the troops of the Soviet Union overran the production facilities of the DKW marque at Zschopau in eastern Germany. Here they found a wealth of special research

and experimental projects as well as standard production components. They transferred completed and unfinished research projects, data and machine tools back to Moscow where it was evaluated at the Central Construction and Experimental Bureau (TsKEB) with a view to using the data and expertise to complete both a production and a racing programme. The head of this bureau, Ing. S Ivanitsky, eventually produced a series of specialised racing machines based on pre-war DKW designs.

The Soviet version of the DKW RT125 was the M-1A. This was raced in the USSR from 1947 onwards in various forms. In 1948 Ivan Ptashkin used one to set a new national speed record for the 125 cc class, nearly 90 kph (54 mph) two-way.

The basic 122.2 cc (52 x 58 mm) three-speed unit construction model was soon improved with redesigned frames and suspension and by engine tuning and closer ratio gears. The S-1A with plunger rear suspension was introduced, and later on specialised racing versions such as the M-IV and M-IE with swinging arm frames were constructed. On a semi-streamlined M-IE, works rider Sergei Kurenkov from the Moscow Torpedo Club attacked a number of Soviet kilometre records in 1950. An interesting feature of this record session was the advanced helmet design employed by Kurenkov. He broke sev-

Above
A pair of DKW-based M-lA racers competing at the Tallinn, Estonia circuit; September 1951

Above right
Sergei Kurenkov on his M-E during a record-breaking session in 1950; he broke several Soviet speeds for the 125 cc class – note his unusual streamlined helmet

Right
Soviet woman racer Hslju Kuunemae on a 15K 350 cc two-stroke twin in August 1951. Hslju was one of several Soviet women competitors who triumphed in motorcycle sport after the Second World War

eral Soviet records, achieving speeds of up to 72 mph – good for what was basically a road-going two-stroke in 1950.

The V A Degtyarev Engineering Works at Kovrov also built racing versions of the Soviet DKW RT125, these being known as the K-125Cl, K-125C2 and K-55C2.

Another DKW-based racer was the S2B; this was a supercharged, four piston, twin cylinder two-stroke, with water-cooling. Although officially credited to Ing. Ivanickeho, it bore all the hallmarks of development by German technicians.

With a capacity of 248.56 cc (33.5 x 70.5 mm) the two cylinders were set vertically side-by-side, and fired at 180 degree intervals. Each cylinder was composed of an inlet and exhaust section, these being angled towards each other at 26 degrees, converging upon a common combustion chamber. As a result of this layout, it had been possible to extend the water-cooling between the two working sections of each cylinder, thus ensuring against distortion. Each piston was flat-topped and a feature of the design was the unusual length of these components. Soviet engineers claimed superior alignment in the bores and improved cooling.

The layout of the bottom half of the S2B engine was extremely interesting. Each 'pair' of induction and exhaust cylinders was carried on its own 180 degree crankshaft assembly, the exhaust crank being more rearwardly placed. It was from this shaft that the primary drive was taken. The shafts were geared together, the pinion teeth being formed on the peripheries of two of the flywheels. These were mated in such a position that the exhaust piston had a considerable lead over the inlet piston, with resulting good scavening and aspiration.

The cylinder barrels and water jacket were of cast iron, a separate light alloy cylinder head being bolted on internally beneath the finned light alloy cover of the water jacket. Circulation of the coolant in the jacket was by the thermosyphon system.

Mounted on the front of the crankcase and fed by an almost vertical 27 mm carburettor was the Centric-type centrifugal supercharger, which had a theoretical output of 760 cc per revolution. This fed mixture into the crankcase, with a spring-loaded poppet relief valve being fitted in the base of the crankcase as a safety measure. With a compression ratio of 6.05:1, the S2B engine produced 40 bhp at 7,200 rpm, giving a maximum speed approaching 115 mph.

As the USSR did not join the FIM until 1 January 1956, supercharging was permitted in Soviet events until that time, several years after it had been banned from the rest of Europe.

Other early post-War Soviet racing machinery included the 350 cc IZh-49 two-stroke and various ohv and ohc four-stroke flat twins ranging from 350 through to 750 cc.

After the country joined the FIM, Soviet riders and designers set about bringing their machines and riding standards up to those of the West. In the summer of 1956 two types of machine appeared in Finland ridden by Viktor Kulakov and Nikolai Sevostianov. These were both dohc twins, the S345 and S555.

Technical details for the S345 included a capacity of 349 cc (60 x 61 mm), 35 bhp at 8,200 rpm, 16 ins

B Populov and A Khomutov piloting their Soviet-built BMW-type sidecar outfit to victory at the Tallinn circuit, September 1954

wheels, telescopic front forks. It had a dry weight of 144 kg (317 lb) and a maximum speed of 102 mph. The larger S555 had over-square bore and stroke dimensions of 72 and 61 mm respectively giving 499 cc, 47 bhp at 7,400 rpm, 19 inch wheels, 150 kg (330 lb) dry weight, Earles type front forks and a maximum speed of 118 mph.

The Soviet team, headed by Ing. A Meshkovsky competed at two Finnish circuits, Elaintarha and Ruissalo, but without much success. The team blamed this lack of results upon wrong gearing for the tight Finnish circuits.

Ing. Meshkovsky commented (rather optimistically) after the racing was over: 'In this visit we have acquired much worth-while knowledge on the grounds of which we shall develop our racing motorcycles into such quality which will be readily comparable with the best American, English, German and Italian trademarks.

The next Soviet racer was the S-157-A, an interesting lightweight for the 125 cc class. This was a double overhead camshaft single with valves set at

Viktor Kulakov with his 499 cc S-555 dohc twin; together with fellow racer Nikolai Sevostianov, he was the first rider from the Soviet Union to compete abroad. The country was Finland, summer 1957

an angle of 50 degrees, measuring 28 mm exhaust and 32 mm inlet. The stroke was rather long at 58.5 mm which with a 46 mm bore, gave a cylinder capacity of 123.6 cc.

When FIM President, Piet Nortier, visited the Central Automoclub headquarters in Moscow during 1959, the chief of the technical department told him that it was not intended to put the S-157-A up to challenge the top Italian lightweights, rather to provide a production racer; and to this purpose a batch of 25 would be constructed towards the end of that year.

Little is known about whether these machines were actually built. The author's feeling is that only a handful of prototypes were constructed, as the next move came with the introduction of the 250 C-259 and 350 C-360 twins.

Kulakov in action at Ruissalo, Finland during 1957

First news of these came on Thursday 11 May 1961 when Nikolai Sevostianov, on a C-360, scored a surprise third place in the 350 class of the Djurgardsloppet international road race held in Helsinki. The race was won by Rhodesian Tommy Robinson (AJS) with Austrian Ladi Richter (Norton) runner-up.

Two Soviet riders (the other being Viktor Pylaev) were competing in Finland as part of the Soviet Union's scheme to develop racing machines and riders which it hoped would be capable of winning world championship class races. At Djurgardsloppet the C-360 proved fast enough to keep Sevostianov ahead of several well-known Scandinavian riders aboard late-type Manx Norton and AJS 7R machinery.

The Finnish appearance was followed in July 1961 when a C-259 racer was displayed as part of the huge three-week Soviet Trade Exhibition at Earls Court, London. The staff claimed 37 bhp at 11,500 rpm on a compression ratio of 10.5:1 and a maximum speed of 120 mph for the Jawa-like dohc twin. Other details included 55 mm bore and 52 mm stroke dimensions, a capacity of 247 cc, six-speed gearbox, a duplex frame, telescopic front forks, swinging arm rear suspension and large diameter full-width alloy brake hubs with two-leading shoe operation both front and rear. Ignition was by coil, with two arm contact breaker and two double-ended coils firing dual

plugs per cylinder. An ingenious feature was the grinding of the springs for the rear suspension units to a barrel shape to provide a progressive rate.

More progress came when Soviet riders and machines made their debut in world championship road racing at the East German Grand Prix held at the Sachsenring in August 1962. Riding the latest version of the C-259, Nikolai Sevostianov finished an excellent fifth in the 250 race; whilst in the 350 he took sixth place after a race-long dice with the Canadian Mike Duff.

At the East German GP the Soviet team manager Konstantin Matujschin revealed that they were busy developing various 125 cc engines including a water-cooled single cylinder two-stroke and a single cylinder four-stroke, but that they 'did not have any intention of contesting the 500 cc class'.

Above right
This 247 cc dohc twin cylinder C-259 racer was displayed at the Soviet Trade Fair, Earls Court, London, 1961

Right
Endel Kiisa's 350 cc Jawa-based twin in the paddock, Dutch TT Assen, 29 June 1963

Into 1963, and the Jawa-based twins made more Grand Prix appearances, Sevostianov finishing fifth in East Germany and fourth in Finland; on both occasions he rode the latest 347.7 cc (59 x 63.6 mm) C-360 which by now produced 53 bhp at 10,800 rpm and was capable of 138 mph on optimum gearing.

Up to this time the Moscow based Central Construction and Experimental Bureau had run their racing programme (since the late 1950s) in collaboration with Motokov of Czechoslovakia. They shared technical information with Jawa and CZ.

Left
The original four-cylinder 350 cc C-364 which caused a minor sensation when it appeared for the first time at the East German GP in July 1964

Below left
Vostok four cylinder engine with gear driven double overhead camshafts followed Italian and Japanese practice

Below
Endel Kiisa in action on the Vostok 350 four at the Austrian Grand Prix, 1 May 1965

This liaison between the two countries was maintained well into the 1960s. From this background the head of the Moscow Bureau, Ing. Ivanitsky and Deputy Director of Laboratories at the VNIImotopram Institute, V Kuznetsov, decided that the time had come to create their own racing design to take on the European and Japanese factories.

Two types were constructed, the 348 cc C-364 and 498 cc C-565. Both were given the same *Boctok* (Vostok) title, a word meaning east or orient. The designation numbers were quite straightforward. The C indicating a sports series machine, the 3 meaning 350 cc, the 5 a 500. The remaining two digits of each number, '64' and '65', showing the date of inception. By applying the above principals the reader will be able to date many of the earlier Soviet racing models already described.

But the really exciting news was that both the C-364 and C-565 were *four* cylinder models. The smaller model was the first to make its bow and when it did so at the East German Grand Prix in July 1964 it caused a minor sensation.

Conventional in design, if somewhat rougher in appearance, this first four cylinder Vostok at that time existed only as a 350, but the 500 was already

on paper. Power output was stated as between 55 and 56 bhp, with a maximum engine speed of 13,000 rpm. The engine was oversquare with bore and stroke dimensions of 49 x 46 mm. Double overhead camshafts, driven by central gear train, followed Italian practice. The six-speed gearbox was in unit with the engine, with a multiplate dry clutch mounted on the nearside. Ignition was via a single coil, situated under the fuel tank, from a low tension magneto.

Both machines retired in the race with piston trouble, after holding third and fourth places behind Redman (Honda) and Havel (Jawa), but not before displaying a performance about equal to the latest works 125 Honda four cylinder racer.

Handling of the machines with telescopic front forks, 19 inch wheels and double-sided twin leading shoe front stoppers was best described as poor, and definitely not up to the standards achieved by the earlier twin cylinder models.

Although this was hardly the type of debut its designers had intended, these machines were to prove the most interesting and technically advanced racing motorcycles that the Soviet Union was ever to produce. They were a clever blend of Soviet-Czech practice, intermixed with ideas from the Gilera/MV Agusta/Benelli/Honda school of thought.

Before going further with the story of the four cylinder Vostoks, it is worth mentioning that at the same 1964 East German GP, Sevostianov rode in the 500 race on an enlarged twin, finishing fourth. Meanwhile the Vostok made one more GP appearance in 1964, when Endel Kiisa finished an excellent third behind Redman and Beale on Hondas in Finland. This was also the best position recorded up to that time by a Soviet entry in the classics.

In 1965 the 350 four appeared in the West German Grand Prix at the Nürburgring, the first championship round of the year. The result was a fifth place by Kiisa. A week later he very nearly scored Russia's first ever international road race victory when leading the 350 cc race in the non-championship Austrian GP on the Vostok four; he retired a mere one-mile from the finish.

Before the East German GP later the same year extensive changes were carried out, with a new frame similar to the Featherbed Norton, in an attempt to cure the previous Camel-like antics. The power unit was also modified, with a new cylinder head assembly, together with the fitment of an oil cooler mounted in the front of the crankcase.

In the race both machines retired, but a week later in the Czech round, Sevostianov finished third behind Redman (Honda) and Woodman (MZ), and in front of the two works Aermacchi singles ridden by Milani and Pasolini.

After this good showing, the Soviets were not seen again until the 1967 Czech GP, where Sevostianov finished fourteenth in the 350 cc race on one of the old twins.

The larger Vostok four cylinder C-565 did not make an appearance outside the Soviet Union until the 1968 Finnish Grand Prix. Of 494 cc the engine showed certain external differences to the original 350 version. It had more fins on the cylinder barrel, a deeper sump and possessed extra finning at the front of the crankcase.

The power output was claimed to be 80 bhp at 12,400 rpm (which appears optimistic) and the dohc engine was similar in construction to the smaller version. Both had pent-roof combustion chambers, four valves per cylinder, ball and roller bearing mounted crankshaft and a deep, finned, alloy sump. The six-speed gearbox, dry multi-plate clutch and duplex tubular frame were more or less identical with the later version of the smaller four. The dry weight of the C-565 was 155 kg (341 lb). A major change was the fitment of the massive drum brakes from the Czech Jawa 350 v-four two-stroke.

Both Sevostianov and Kiisa were aboard the large Vostoks for the 500 race. At the end of the first lap Kiisa was 1.5 seconds behind the race leader Giacomo Agostini riding the factory MV Agusta. On lap three, Kiisa accelerated past the Italian world champion out of a slow corner and a Soviet machine led a 500 cc Grand Prix for the first and only time in racing history. Unfortunately this moment of glory lasted only briefly and Agostini soon retook the lead and drew away, while Kiisa had to retire on the fourth lap with engine trouble. Sevostianov brought the other Vostok home in fourth position behind Agostini, Jack Findlay (McIntyre Matchless) and Derek Woodman (Seeley G50).

In 1969, the final Grand Prix appearance of the four cylinder Vostok came in the 500 race over the Sachsenring circuit in East Germany. Kiisa was there together with a new team-mate, Juri Randla, and both had modified engines. The new motors featured completely revised top ends with the cylinder heads sporting *three* valves per cylinder – two exhaust and one inlet. The Soviets claimed a realistic 75 bhp at 12,200 rpm.

Kiisa (left) with Nikolai Sevostianov and the 500 C-565 four at the 1965 East German GP. Note massive front brake on the larger model

In a wet race, and after holding third for a while Randla retired with carburation problems. Kiisa on the second Vostok pressed on at a slower pace and came home tenth after a lengthy pit stop to change a plug. Both riders and machines appeared a week later in the Czech GP at Brno, but both retired on the second lap with sick engines.

After a gap of three years the Soviets made a surprise return to world championship racing at the East German Grand Prix in July 1972. They fielded three 50 cc and two 125 cc machines under the Riga name. In the smaller class two of their three riders,

Eduard Borisenko and Alexander Smertien, finished in seventh and eleventh places. As no other Soviet machines ever appeared in a world championship event again it can only be surmised that they had finally realised that it was going to be far more difficult to defeat the might of Europe and Japan than they had originally thought.

All this was two decades and more ago; who knows what the new era of democracy now sweeping what remains of the vast Soviet empire may bring in the 1990s, thanks to the process of *glasnost* and *perestroika* begun by the Gorbachov regime?

6
Spain

Land of bullfights, siesta and sunshine, Spain did not look upon the motorcycle as anything more than a sportsman's toy until the mid-1940s. Then the country changed its outlook and the two-wheel motorisation era was born. The Spanish, once underway, rapidly built up a thriving motorcycle industry and with it a vibrant interest (read passion) for the sport, notably road racing.

In many ways, as I outlined in my earlier book *Spanish Postwar Road and Racing Motorcycles* (Osprey), the birth of the motorcycle industry in that country was almost entirely due to the Second World War. In the years following the end of the Spanish Civil War (1936–39) the rest of Europe was involved in its own, much larger conflict. But for Spain, attempting to rebuild itself, the Second World War meant a desperate shortage of imported goods – and especially transport. It was therefore impossible to buy-in vehicles from abroad and the vast majority of those which had survived the domestic conflict in Spain were now old and in very poor condition.

The situation was so acute that for the first time, Spaniards wondered whether they themselves might produce powered transport. It was in this climate that two young industrialists, Pedro Permanyer and Francisco Bulto – both keen motorcyclists – joined forces with the express purpose of manufacturing a small two-wheeler with which to meet the needs of the time. And so came into existence Montesa, the founding member of an industry which over the next four decades was to build up into a major force in world motorcycling, before entering a period of decline and ultimate collapse during the 1980s. During the same period Spanish motorcycles and riders came to the forefront in racing, but whereas Spanish marques virtually disappeared in the 1980s, its riders and even more so its fans have attained an ever-growing influence.

Bultaco

There can be few of the world's motorcycle marques which owe their origin to the events of another company's board meeting. None, perhaps, except Bultaco.

In May 1958 a meeting of directors was called at Montesa, then the largest of Spain's motorcycle factories. There had been heated disputes for some time over a single, central issue – to race or not to race – and this meeting was to prove the final straw.

The two key figures at the centre of the disagreement were the factory's founders, both not only directors but major shareholders. Francisco Xavier Bulto and Pedro Permanyer were men whose partnership had seemed ideal when they had founded Montesa in 1945. Now they found themselves at opposite sides of completely unreconcilable views. Permanyer, the majority shareholder, was backed by the other Montesa directors in his opinion that the factory should withdraw completely from racing for the same economic reasons that had influenced other factories. To Bulto, the firm's racing involvement and reputation was all-important and without it he saw no future for Montesa.

The May meeting proved to be the watershed. Bulto, now aged 46, left Montesa, intending to devote his time and energy to other business interests, in the shape of a textile plant and a piston manufacturing concern. It was not to be. Learning of Bulto's departure, most of Montesa's racing department followed suit and within a few days the 'old man' received an invitation to dinner with several of his former technical staff, mechanics and riders. There, Bulto's ex-employees pleaded with him to start a brand-new motorcycle concern – one which could follow through their shared love for the sport.

Impressed as much by their enthusiasm as their logic, Bulto agreed to set about the huge task of creating a completely new name within the Spanish industry at a time when so many others were foundering, and when even mighty Montesa were feeling the pinch. Despite their love of racing, all those at the meeting were only too well aware that they would only survive if their machines were commercially profitable – and that meant that they had to build roadsters. On 3 June 1958, a group of 12 former Montesa engineers met Bulto at his home. The purpose of this meeting was to discuss the design of a brand-new 125 cc road bike, which could not only be sold in satisfactory numbers as a means of transport, but would also form the basis of a simple, effective racing iron.

Later that month, the embryonic company moved to a farm owned by Bulto at San Adrian de Besos on the northern outskirts of Barcelona. Conditions there were spartan in the extreme, especially for an engineering-based company. The offices were in the farm outbuildings, many of which were crumbling with age and disrepair. Engineering facilities were even more primitive: for example, the lathe and other machine tools were set up with only a roof to cover them so far as was essential for production purposes.

It took four months for the design team, headed by Sr. Bulto himself, to conclude its work and so turn the initial design sketches into metal. Himself a keen and active motorcyclist, Bulto often rode the proto-types to assist with the road test programme.

By February 1959, development work on the first design had been completed and a press day was planned to launch the new marque's first product. Only one detail was lacking – a suitable name for the farmyard company.

Johnny Grace, works rider and engineer, was the man who supplied the answer by using a combination of Bulto and Paco (a Spanish nickname for Francisco) – hence Bult/aco. The origins of the famous 'thumbs-up' symbol on the company badge were equally fortuitous. Bulto himself conceived the logo after he witnessed British rider David Whitworth giving a thumbs-up signal to his pit crew. Asking what this meant, he was told that it signified that all was well. From that moment on, it appeared on all Bultaco machinery.

The machine which was launched to the press was the Tralla 101 (in English the name translates literally to 'whiplash'). It was to prove an excellent little machine, with good performance and reliability in service helping to establish the company both financially and in the eyes of those of the public

Bultaco 'factory' circa 1960 – outbuildings at Snr Bulto's farm!

Bultaco's first racing effort was in 1960 with stripped down 125 cc roadsters. Johnny Grace in the saddle

who invested their money. The engine was a two-stroke single with piston port induction. From a capacity of 124 cc it gave 12 bhp at 6,000 rpm, using a 22 mm Dell'Orto carburettor, 10.5:1 compression ratio and dimensions of 51.5 x 60 mm, bore and stroke. There was a steel conrod with the big-end in a double-row caged roller bearing, and a unit four-speed gearbox with chain primary drive. Typical of lightweights of the period, the ignition system (and lighting) was powered by a 6-volt flywheel magneto.

The technical details added up to give a performance of 71 mph. And of course, with Bultaco's sporting instincts, certain 'performance' extras were also offered, including close ratio gears and alternative sprockets. The standard ratio was 15/48 teeth, but there were also 14 and 16 tooth gearbox sprockets, and 46, 50, 52 and 54 for the rear wheel. Also on offer were clip-on handlebars, a tank rubber cushion, and an expansion chamber exhaust system. The Tralla 101 offered a good combination of sporting performance, safe handling and comfort. In its first production year, it was to sell a total of 1,136 units.

Just two months after the company's official

launch, Bultaco entered its first racing event. This was the roadster class (based on the popular Italian Formula racing series) at the 1959 Spanish Grand Prix. It was a highly successful debut for the firm, with a pack of Bultacos finishing in 2nd, 3rd, 4th, 5th, 7th, 8th and 9th places. Appropriately, the highest placed Bultaco rider was none other than Johnny Grace, who finished a hair's breadth behind the winning Montesa – although this was not, of course, a factory entry.

Spurred on by this encouraging start, the team then decided to modify a standard Tralla 101 by replacing the standard 22 mm carburettor with a larger, 29 mm Dell'Orto SS1, tuning the engine, and fitting a pukka racing expansion chamber. No-one could have known at the time, but this set of modifications was to lead directly to the birth of the famous TSS racing machines.

The specially-tuned bike was entered in the important late-season Spanish international races at Madrid in October. In a field including some much more expensive works machinery, the little two-stroke single with Marcello Cama aboard came home in 6th spot.

The following week, at Zaragoza, the Bultaco team entered the production class. This was simply because they believed that the piston port single would be hopelessly outclassed in the open class, where it would be up against such machines as the MV Agusta ridden by world champion Carlo Ubbiali, and Bruno Spaggiari's desmo Ducati.

However, the race organisers over-ruled Bultaco's wishes; since in their judgement the machines were 'too noisy' to qualify for the production class, the open class it must be. The Bultaco mechanics worked flat-out throughout the night before the race in a desperate attempt to convert their road bikes into racers. As day dawned, the work was complete, but the team were apprehensive of the race's outcome.

As the bikes were wheeled out onto the tarmac, the tension mounted, but almost as soon as the flag dropped, it was as if God were on the side of Bultaco. Out of nowhere, the rain came down with ever-increasing force and soon the whole circuit was awash. On the wet, slippery surface, an amazing spectacle unfolded; for the light, peppy Bultacos were able to out-corner the more powerful, but heavier, four-strokes.

In an attempt to get ahead of the angry swarm of 'strokers, Spaggiari came to grief and got to know the tarmac at close quarters – followed two laps later by none other than the multiple world champion Ubbiali. In the ensuing crash, Johnny Grace, who

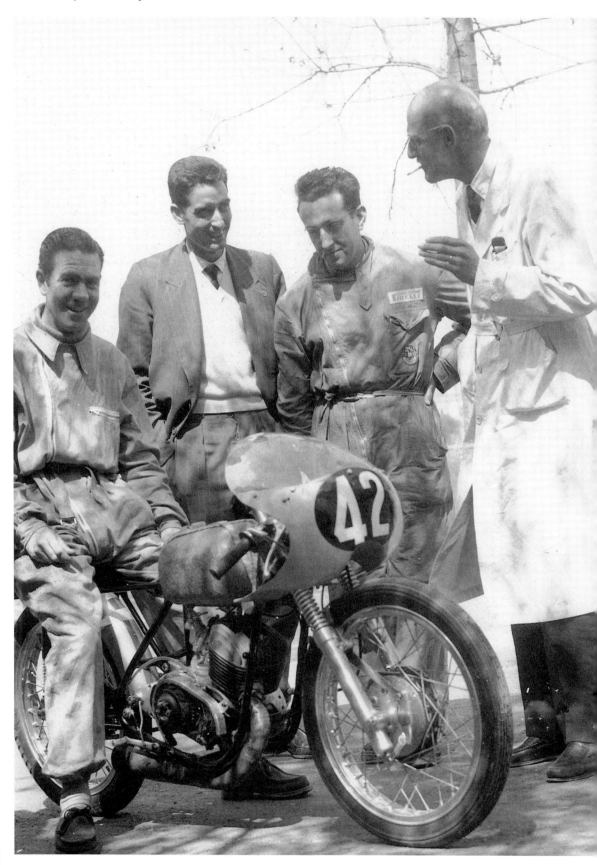

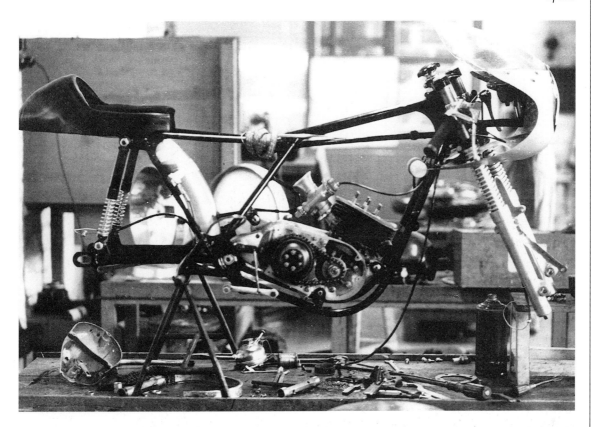

Bultaco's first racing machine as used in the 1960 Spanish GP; showing sturdy duplex frame, leading axle front forks, steeply inclined carb and chain primary drive

was right behind the Italian, also ran into trouble; but Marcello Cama, riding another Bultaco virtually on the back wheel of Grace's machine went on to score a totally unexpected but thoroughly popular win for the team – thumbs-up, indeed!

This victory in a world-class contest so early in their career gave the green light to Bultaco's plans to develop their first production racer – the four speed TSS 125. Throughout 1960, prototypes of this machine were raced at home and abroad by a team of factory riders, including Grace, Cama and Quintanilla. Amongst other important events, their programme included a debut in the Isle of Man TT, and it was not to be long before derivatives would be on general sale.

Another significant milestone for Bultaco came in October 1960 when a machine with a specially prepared engine was taken to Montlhéry in France with the objective of breaking a number of long distance speed records.

The engine was a 175 (174.77 cc) based on the

smaller unit, and specially developed in the factory's race shop. With dimensions of 60.9 x 60 mm, it ran on a 9:1 compression ratio and produced 18 bhp at 8,000 rpm. The engine had a four-speed gearbox, and was later to form the basis of the 196 and 244 cc engines used to power a variety of roadsters, as well as racers, scramblers and even go-karts.

The record-breaker had a sleek, streamlined fairing, almost completely covering the whole bike. This enabled the machine to reach a top speed a shade over 107 mph; and on the high-banked speed bowl at Montlhéry, the 175 Bultaco streamliner was capable of attaining flying lap speeds of up to 105 mph.

The riders for the record attempt, which took place on 1 and 2 October, were Johnny Grace (the team leader), Marcello Cama, Ricardo Quintanilla, Francisco Gonzales, and the veteran Frenchman Georges Monneret. Their first attempt was on the 12-hour record, where for ten hours the streamliner ran superbly – averaging well over 90 mph. But then a major problem appeared, in the shape of a broken

Preparing for the 1960 Spanish GP. Left to right, Johnny Grace (on bike), a Spanish journalist, Alberto Numen (chief engineer) and Snr Bulto. The machine is the company's first pukka racer

frame tube. Johnny Grace called for an inspection of the trouble, but then decided to take the Bultaco out again to complete the time schedule, and complete the world record at 89.27 mph.

Following this, a new frame was essential, and 1½ hours were spent on repairs. After sterling work by the pit crew during which the whole bike was virtually reassembled, the team went out again to break the 24-hour record at an average speed of 81.81 mph. Amazingly enough, this was also enough to take the 250 and 350 classes as well, records which stood unchallenged for a number of years afterwards. Finally, in a fitting finale to a great outing, Monneret went out and rolled off six laps, each one at an average speed of over 100 mph.

Towards the end of the year, moves were made to import the Bultaco range into Britain. John Aneley, a leading dealer based in Blackburn, Lancashire was

Left
Bultaco broke 5 long distance world records at the French Montlhery circuit in October 1960 with his specially prepared 175 cc streamliner. Left to right: Ricardo Quintanilla, Marcelo Cama, Paco Gonzales, Snr Bulto and Johnny Grace.

Below
First Bultaco production racer, the 1962 125 TSS. 124.98 cc (51.5 × 60 mm) 21 bhp at 10,500 rpm. Maximum speed over 110 mph

appointed sole UK importer for the Spanish machines and immediately formed Bultaco Concessionaires Ltd, whose premises were at King Street, Blackburn. Aneley was previously responsible for building the Aneley Special, a 125 cc racer not unlike the Montesa of the mid-1950s so was well versed in the ways of both small two-strokes and racing. Aneley had first met Sr. Bulto when, as Montesa race boss, he had visited the Isle of Man for the 1956 TT. The new company's sales manager was none other than Ken Martin, a well-known lightweight road racing exponent of the day who was later to campaign various Bultacos with a fair measure of success, including winning the Scottish 200 championship on the 196 cc TSS in 1962.

Shortly after Bultaco Concessionaires was founded, John Aneley approached Dan Shorey, a leading lightweight rider at the time, with the offer of a factory-prepared TSS 125 to race in the 1961 British championships, then known as the ACU Star series. Shorey recalls that he 'didn't need asking twice'; however development difficulties with the 1961 bikes held his machine over in Spain until Easter. This forced Shorey to drive down through France himself, together with Tommy Robb, to pick up the TSS from Bultaco's Barcelona factory. He made it back to Britain with six days to spare before his first ride, and was rewarded for his troubles and effort with a 3rd place in the Bultaco's debut race at Brands Hatch, Kent on 30 March. Shorey's first win

on the Bultaco was at Aberdare Park on 13 May 1961. There followed wins and lap records all over Britain, culminating at the end of the season with winning the British championship. This was the coveted ACU Gold Star. A lasting memory for Dan Shorey was when 'Sr. Bulto's face lit up on seeing the ACU Star I had won on my Bultaco. 'He kept it on his desk for a whole year, until it had to be returned.'

The other 'works supported' Bultaco 125 in Britain during 1961 was that sponsored by Geoff Monty and ridden by Tommy Robb. Outside of Spain itself these two riders were the first of many.

Left
Ulsterman Tommy Robb was an early convert to Bultaco machinery. He's seen here in action on an air-cooled 125 at Oulton Park in April 1961

Below left
Another British rider, Don Shorey, campaigned Bultacos with considerable success. His 1961 machine is shown in factory fresh condition early that year

Below
Ross Insley with his standard production four-speed air-cooled 125 TSS at Mallory Park, April 1962

After the success of the works TSS racers, a highlight of 1961 was when the first TSS 125 production racers went on sale to the public. The specification of the production model closely followed the bikes officially raced by the factory, with a power output of 20 bhp at 10,300 rpm from the 124.98 cc engine (51.5 x 60 mm bore and stroke, 13.5:1 compression ratio).

The alloy cylinder head had a central 14 mm sparking plug and squish-type combustion chamber. Also in alloy, the barrel had a precision centrifugally-cast iron liner, and carried a Mahle piston with two L-type rings – the upper ring in direct contact with the combustion chamber. A full flywheel crankshaft was carried in two ball races, and both big and small ends were German INA roller bearings. The big-end had ten full-width 2 mm caged rollers, and the outer race was formed directly in the con-rod eye. The small end had separate needle rollers and gave a much greater standard of reliability and free running than the conventional bronze bush.

Ignition, as on the roadsters, was provided by a Femsa flywheel magneto, number 201–1. This had a conventional built-in low tension coil and contact breaker points on the stator plate, and an external HT coil which was mounted under the fuel tank. The

carburettor was a Spanish Arbeo – actually a licence-built Dell'Orto SSl 29A – carried at 26 degrees off the vertical and using a remote float chamber.

The production machines had only a four-speed gearbox (six gears were used on the works bikes from early 1962) but there were variable internal ratios to keep the engine on the boil, enabling its pilot to obtain optimum performance. Primary drive was a 52-pitch Renold 11038 chain running in an oil bath chaincase which also housed the all-metal multiplate clutch, while final drive was also by Renold chain, 11046, with 130 pitches.

The 'blacksmith' look of the production TSS's frame has come in for some criticism over the years. Unlike the works machines, which used high quality 16-gauge steel tube, it was constructed to much heavier, but weaker, 10 swg ($\frac{1}{8}$ in. wall thickness) 'gas piping' of poor quality. That said, it was actually a fantastic handler. On top, it carried a 14-litre fibreglass fuel tank secured by a single central strap, and a fibreglass seat covered in chamois leather.

The wheels had alloy hubs with a full-width 160 mm front brake with air scoop, and 140 mm conical rear brake. The rims were alloy, by Akront, and carried 2.75 x 18 in Spanish licence-built Pirelli MT roadster tyres – a block rear and ribbed front.

Dry weight was a low 78 kg (171.6 lb) despite the

Details of the 'over-the-counter' 1962 125 TSS; its chunky engine . . .

quite heavy frame, and as delivered, the TSS came complete with a neat, racing dolphin fairing. One notable omission was a rev counter. The British price when the machine was launched early in 1961 was £370.16s.4d., some £70 more than originally forecast.

Despite the price and a few shortcomings, the TSS soon proved to be the best machine available to private owners in its class. Just one of its achievements in that first season included a 6th in the Ultra Lightweight Isle of Man TT, ridden by Ralph Renson (a personal friend of Johnny Grace), at an average of 83.26 mph to gain Bultaco's first ever leaderboard placing in an IoM TT race – Renson was incidentally the first rider home on anything other than a works Honda. By the end of the season, TSS models had also succeeded in capturing the national championships in Spain, Argentina, Uraguay and of course, Britain.

Undoubtedly, 1962 was a particularly important year for Bultaco, with many new roadsters, together with a series of Kart engines.

Meanwhile, back in the motorcycle racing arena, the simple piston port two-strokes were continuing

to make increasing inroads into the record books, even at world championship level. Not only had the 125 category fallen to the Barcelona factory, but they had now successfully challenged the 250 class as well. In addition to his TSS 125, Dan Shorey now had a 196 cc model. The instigator of the 200 cc racer project was in fact Ken Martin, who at the back-end of 1961 had asked for a 175. What he got was a 196, a development of the K200 then being finished for production as a racing kart engine. The main difference was the repositioning of the exhaust port to give slightly later opening. The 196 cc engine had a four-speed gearbox, similar to the one used on the production version of the TSS 125; unlike the works 125, which by then was a six-speed design.

With the larger mount, Shorey achieved several excellent results, including some fine Grand Prix performances. The first of these was at the first GP of the year – fortuitously, the Spanish round at Mont-juich Park in Barcelona. Here Shorey achieved a 4th position, behind the three works Honda fours of Redman, McIntyre and Phillis. He repeated this achievement with a carbon-copy result in the French GP at Clermont Ferrand, the next round. Before the start of the race, Shorey found himself alongside Bob

. . . 'gas pipe' frame tubing (above) . . .

. . . and conical rear wheel hub (below)

McIntyre on the front row of the grid. With a typically straight-to-the-point comment the Honda works rider burst out 'Oh no, not you and that bloody thing again!'

With Bultaco lying 4th after two rounds of the championship, the circus then moved to the Isle of Man for the TT. Here, the little two-stroke would be at more of a disadvantage, as with such a long way to go, the air-cooled single would begin to tire before the end of the race. Even so, Shorey finished 6th in a race which was won by Honda Britain's rider Derek Minter, with McIntyre retiring, Redman in 2nd, and Phillis 3rd (it was rumoured at the time that by not observing 'team' orders, Minter invoked the wrath of senior Honda management back in Japan, and so jeopardised his chances of becoming a full 'works' rider). The other machines between the Japanese and the Spanish were two Italians: a Guzzi ridden by veteran privateer Arthur Wheeler, and the factory Aermacchi of Alberto Pagani.

Except for another 6th, at the East German GP at the Sachsenring, Shorey and the 196 cc Bultaco did not make any further showing in the points for the 1962 250 cc world championship. Despite this, Bultaco still managed to finish 7th overall. The 196 cc TSS had proved itself to be outstandingly reliable, so that the machine's total spares requirements for the season amounted to a single big-end and piston. And this was backed by a surprising turn of speed, with 128 mph being recorded during the 250 TT (while the TSS 125 was good for 117 mph).

Meanwhile, the 125 class saw points gained by Argentinian rider Jorge Kissling, 6th at the French GP and Johnny Grace, 5th in the West German GP at Solitude. 4th and 5th places were also gained in the final round staged at the Buenos Aires autodrome, where the Bultacos were entered by a couple of local riders.

Bultacos did even better at national level, winning championship titles in Peru, Argentina, Sweden, France and Britain. In Britain, Bultaco and Dan Shorey were double champions, winning both the ACU 125 and 250 titles, and leaving no doubt at the time that 'Banbury Dan' was Bultaco's finest rider. For good measure, British importer Bultaco Concessionaires' sales manager Ken Martin won the Scottish 200 cc championship. And at home, while the Spanish 125 cc championship was won by Ducati-

Fred Hardy at Waterworks during the 1962 125 cc TT. Thirty years on this Isle of Man view has gone, obscured by the trees

mounted Bruno Spaggiari, on loan to the Spanish Ducati arm, Mototrans, he was hotly pursued by two Bultaco riders, Francisco Gonzales and a young rider named Ramon Torras who had only joined the factory team at the beginning of the year.

Other notable sporting achievements of 1962 included a win in the 125 cc class of the Barcelona 24 Hours endurance race, and a pair of gold medals in the ISDT held at Garmisch, West Germany. Prophetic stuff, this, with a fore-taste of future Bultaco successes in off-road events.

Bultaco was not about to rest on its laurels and plenty of development work was underway. One important innovation which the Spanish factory were instrumental in bringing to the fore was the use of a new contactless self-generating electronic ignition. This was designed by Femsa during 1962–3, and was first tried out on the Bultaco factory's 'works' racers. It was later incorporated on the production TSS 125 model and this type of ignition has since become the standard equipment of virtually every two-stroke racer, playing a major part in making the modern two-stroke as reliable as it has become.

196 cc Bultaco; chain primary drive, Amal GP carb and cast iron cylinder

In the winter of 1962–3, the majority of Bultaco's efforts went into improving and extending the TSS road racing range. The 125 cc model received a power boost to 24 bhp at 10,300 rpm. This was achieved by increasing the compression ratio to 14:1, improving the crankcase sealing and fitting a remote float chamber. The big-end was strengthened.

There was also a new model. The success of Shorey's development 196 cc model had spurred the factory on to build a batch of production models alongside the already well-established smaller version. The production 196 used the same 29 mm Spanish-made Dell'Orto SS1 carburettor as was fitted to the 125, but although this meant that its power was only 6 bhp more than the smaller machine (30 at 9,500 rpm), its excellent power-to-weight ratio endowed it with sufficient performance not to be outclassed against a full 250 – being in effect a 125 in all its important dimensions, but with a 50 per cent increase in capacity.

British importer Bultaco Concessionaires listed three TSS models for 1963 – two versions of the 125, and the new 200. The difference between the two 125s was mainly in the gearbox, for one used the four-speed design, while the other had the trouble-some six-speeder. Complete with fairing, but less sprockets and rev-counter, the four-speeder cost £325, while the fairing equipped six-speeder had both sprockets and rev-counter included in its price of £399. The fully-equipped four-speed TSS 196 cost a little less at £370.

The introduction to the concessionaires' specification sheets for the three models noted; 'During the past racing season great strides have been taken in an endeavour to improve what is accepted in the racing world as probably the most successful racing lightweight generally available today ... The probabilities of winning any of the classic races counting for the World Championships are remote. However, it should provide you with enjoyment and stand a reasonable chance of success in any other event, in which official representative teams are not participating'. This was accurate and truthful, and quite unlike the hype often put out to publicise motorcycling products today.

The 1963 season started well enough, with a headline-grabbing victory by Ramon Torras at Modena, Italy. Pitted in the 125 class against many of the world's leading riders mounted on the best works bikes, the works air-cooled six-speed Bultaco overcame the whole field to record perhaps the factory's finest victory up to that time. The second man home was multiple world champion Jim Redman, on the works Honda.

Following this giant-killing demonstration of the Bultaco's ability, many enthusiasts could well have been forgiven for thinking that 1963 would be a year of victory for the Spanish bikes on the world's race tracks. In fact, it was to prove the poorest season of the period.

In the 250 cc world championships, bikes such as the improved Honda four, the fabulously rapid Morini single, and the newly introduced Yamaha twins, left Bultaco unable to gain even a point. Quite simply, the war of rapid technological development which was being waged between Bultaco's larger rivals meant that the 196 cc engine had been outstripped within 12 months of its launch.

The smaller machines fared better in the 125 class, with 5th and 6th places during the opening Grand Prix at Barcelona, scored by Francisco Gonzales jun. and Canadian Mike Duff respectively. A 6th at the Belgian GP by Frenchman J P Beltoise was followed by the first appearance of a new water-cooled machine ridden by Johnny Grace at the Italian GP, staged at Monza during September – the high spot for the Spanish factory of what was, for them, an otherwise drab season. After a race-long duel with the Italian Guiseppe Visenzi, mounted on the Honda CR93, Grace finished 5th, ahead of Stanislov Malina on a works CZ four-stroke single. The race was won by Honda works rider Luigi Taveri. Another noteworthy Bultaco works rider of the period was American Jess Thomas, who was also one of the first of his countrymen to join the 'Continental Circus'.

Water-cooling the Bultaco single was an obvious step for the factory to take, the main advantage being less power loss when the engine got hot. Internally, the design was much as before, but there was now a totally new barrel and cylinder head. The barrel was unfinned, and carried stubs for attaching the hoses from a small radiator which was mounted ahead of the engine. In order to accommodate this, the single front downtube of the frame was replaced by widely-splayed duplex tubes.

The Grand Prix season was rounded off for Bultaco with 2nd and 3rd places in the 125 cc Argentinian GP behind the winner Jim Redman. The riders were Pochettino and Caldarella – the latter was to win worldwide fame a few short months later for his fiery performances aboard the 500 Gilera four in pursuit of Mike Hailwood's four-cylinder MV, culminating with a 2nd place in the Italian GP at Monza.

By comparison, 1962 hero Dan Shorey had a miserable season, and although wins came at national level, the level of retirements shot up alarmingly. The truth of the matter was that to stay competitive, the factory were taking extreme measures to search for that elusive additional power so desperately needed to stay at the front of the pack. Unlike his previous experiences with Bultaco, Shorey recalls that 'engines came and went' and his view expressed in typically plain language was that: 'the factory was messing about'.

Even though he had tried hard enough, Shorey found that his bid to retain the British 125 championship was thwarted by Dave Simmonds' 125 Tohatsu twin, Rex Avery on Joe Erhlich's EMC single and Tommy Robb, now mounted on a Honda CR93. The 196 cc machine was just not competitive enough, except in events such as the separate 200 cc class races held in Scotland and Ireland.

Even though the pure racing models had a less than successful year, some fine performances were put up by the 200 Metralla sports model in production races throughout Spain. The Barcelona 24

Hours was just one such venue, where the fleet 200 sportsters gained some impressive results. Bultaco also sent works riders to foreign events such as the British Thruxton 500-miler, and by the end of the season Bultaco had class winners in the European *Grand Prix d'Endurance* trophy, an outstanding achievement when giving away 50 cc to all their four-stroke rivals.

Meanwhile, work was underway to update the TSS racing models. The machines which were planned to turn things round for Bultaco were water-cooled versions of both the 125 and a brand-new 250 engine. The water-cooling was based on the prototype which had appeared at Monza in 1963, and the work was headed by chief engineer Alberto Numen. The intention was to use 1964 as a development period, with the real push coming in 1965; although several of the 1964 works machines carried water-cooling, and the prototype 250 was raced in several events, the production machines were all air-cooled.

The 125 was now only available in the six-speed version and was purely a development of the previous year's model. But while the 250 obviously borrowed some parts from the TSS 200, it was virtually brand-new. With a capacity of 244 cc, it used a bore and stroke of 72 x 60 mm, had a five-speed gearbox and a new duplex frame, allowing the use of a central exhaust port for the first time. But although it was fast, the 250 tended to suffer piston seizures. It also had a real Achilles heel, in the shape of the chain primary drive, now being taken to the absolute limit. Unless the chain was replaced at very frequent intervals, the result would be quite simple – it would snap!

Grand Prix placings were once again scarce for Bultaco in 1964: only one in the 250 class, a 3rd by the American Bo Gehring on a TSS 200 in the opening US Grand Prix at Daytona, behind Alan Shepherd's MZ twin and ex-patriate Englishman Ron Grant's Parilla. In the 125, J P Beltoise gained two 5th places in the French and US events, and Ramon Torras rode superbly against a horde of Japanese works machinery to take 6th place in the Ulster Grand Prix over the Dundrod circuit.

The highlight of 1965 was the introduction of the 125 and 250 water-cooled road racers, which made

1963 Isle of Man TT. Dan Shorey 9th on his works 196 cc Bultaco

New Zealander Ginger Molloy at Thruxton in early 1965 with his 244 cc air-cooled Bultaco

it possible for a whole string of Bultaco riders, both factory and private entrants, to notch up a host of racing successes that year.

Without doubt, the finest result amongst several excellent finishes in that year's Grands Prix was works rider Ramon Torras, who succeeded in splitting the works Yamaha RD56 twins of winner Phil Read and Mike Duff at the Spanish 250 GP held around the twisting Montjuich Park, Barcelona. At the time, the Yamahas were the fastest machines in the class, and for one to be beaten by a machine as outwardly simple as the Bultaco was nothing short of amazing.

As a further testament to the handling qualities of the bike, and the skill of its rider, Torras also scored two 3rds at the West German GP at the Nürburgring. With an electrifying performance in the 125 race, he finished in front of the Suzuki rider Ernst Degner, and the MZ of Derek Woodman, both of them with ultra-rapid specialised works machinery.

Other points gained in the 125 class for the 1965 season were Gehring's 6th in the US GP at Daytona, Tommy Robb's 6th in the Ulster, and Ginger Molloy's 6th at Monza. In the 250, Barry Smith was 3rd

in the French at Rouen, with J C Guenard 4th and Rex Avery fifth. Ginger Molloy was 6th again in the Ulster and 4th in the Italian (ahead of Franta Stastny's CZ and Gunter Beer's Honda four). Bob Coulter was 6th in the Finnish GP at Imatra.

At the IoM TT, works-supported rider Australian Kevin Cass got his 125 around at an average of 81.98 mph. But considering Johnny Grace's speed of 83 mph two years before on an air-cooled machine, one could be left to wonder if the water-cooled bikes were any quicker. The truth of the matter was that the air-cooled machine was just as fast but not forlong, tiring and slowing over a long race. Watercooling simply prolonged the peak performance.

A notable British result was Tommy Robb's ride in the North West 200, staged in Northern Ireland – a mixture of a speed event and round-the-houses handling test. Robb's winning performance proved that, outside GP events, the new water-cooled 250 Bultaco could better just about anything else on the road.

Both models were physically similar, with a dry weight of 86 kg (198 lb) including fairings. Both had 13-litre tanks and a 2-litre radiator capacity. The wheels were 18 ins front and rear with a 2.50 ins front tyre and 2.75 ins rear. They also shared many engine and ancillary components, including six-speed gearboxes, chain primary drive and the all-metal plate clutch running in an oil bath. The carburettors on both were 30 mm Spanish Amal 389 GPs.

The 124.98 cc engine had 51.5 x 60 mm dimensions and a compression ratio of 13.5:1, with Femsa electronic ignition and an additional lubrication system in which a manual tap supplied 10 to 12 drops of oil per minute. It gave 27 bhp at 11,000 rpm, measured at the crank. The 244.2 cc engine had a larger bore of 72 mm, a compression ratio of 11.75:1 and gave 38 bhp at 9,500 rpm (crankshaft figures). There was no additional lubrication, and the absolute maximum permissible revs were 9,800, although 9,500 was a safe sustained limit.

After 1964, the British imports were handled by Rickman Brothers (Engineering) Ltd of New Milton, Hampshire. The original tie-up between them and Bultaco had been the use of Don and Derek's Rickman Metisse frame for the Bultaco motocross engine, but they were also keen on road racing. Their list of 'Useful Hints' to ensure that private owners of the water-cooled TSS achieved the best possible reliability remains the most definitive statement of what ownership meant, and is worth recording in its entirety:

We supply the TSS with Pirelli tyres. These are not proper racing tyres and we recommend that you fit either Avon or Dunlop racing tyres 2.50 x 18 front and 2.75 x 18 rear. The road holding properties of the machine will be improved on bends, and it will also increase slightly its top speed.

If, after a few races, you notice that the engine has lost its acceleration and has a tendency to show the same symptoms as when the carburettor floods, it is almost certain the needle jet (jet holder) has worn and is oval. Replace the part with a new one, size 105.

It is always advisable to check the bolts fixing the rear wheel sprocket to the hub.

If castor oil is used in the machine, care should be taken to make sure the mixing has been properly carried out. There are some petrols which do not mix very happily with this type of oil. Low temperatures make mixing very difficult.

If your engine does not stop when you shut off the throttle and you have checked that the carburettor slide is bottoming, then it is almost certain that the crankcase oil seal on the flywheel magneto side is badly worn. Replace!

The additional lubrication tap (125) should be opened as late as possible before the start, or otherwise as soon as possible after having started. It would be advisable to close it after the race before stopping the engine.

A couple of interesting racer tests of the works-supported New Zealander Ginger Molloy's 125 and 250 were carried out by *Motor Cycling* in their 1 and 22 May 1965 issues respectively. The machines were from a small batch of specially prepared production models, on which the standard parts included an Oldani front brake on the 250, Amal GP 'matchbox' type float chambers, and Girling rear suspension units.

Under the heading 'Preparation', Molloy noted that although simple to tune and ride, 'all Bultacos respond to careful preparation'. Listing important points to watch, he singled out the primary chain, 'which must be replaced regularly', and the rear chain, which 'runs very hot and it is important to adjust it so slack that it will just touch, when lightly pressed, the top of the pivot tube'. Although the Femsa electronic ignition was excellent, 'regular replacement of the timing side oil seal is required. It runs dry. If it fails, the timing unit gets soaked in oil'. Although carburation often needed special setting for a particular meeting, the Spanish Amal had improved in one aspect, 'we are no longer continually chasing the settings to compensate for wear', although plug chops to ascertain the correct mixture were recommended. Tyre pressures were a matter of personal taste, but seemed best at 22/24 psi front and rear, and Molloy noted, 'it is not really necessary to drop these figures for a wet day'.

Before revving the engine (Molloy used the word 'bombed') he said 'the motor must get hot. The motor goes best if it is not over-cooled as it can be on a cold day. But blanking off some of the radiator is easy'. In fact, the optimum working water temperature for a racing TSS is 85 degrees C (185 degrees F). Ridden under 70 degrees C (158 degrees F), the engine could 'cold' seize – be warned!

Molloy had similar comments to make about the 250, emphasising plug chops and chain maintenance and noting on this one that: 'the contact breaker gap is critical; it must be 17 thou – but it will keep that setting'. Reassuringly, he summed up the brace of Bultacos as 'straight-forward, with very little work for me between meetings'. He had amply proved his point with victory at the Saar GP in 1964, and international wins in France and Sweden, as well as the

Water-cooled 125 TSS at 1965 IoM TT. The prototype of this machine had made its debut in the hands of factory race tester Johnny Grace at the Italian GP back in September 1963; but it didn't reach production until some 18 months later

Above
Bultaco Metrallas dominated the 250 cc class of the 1967 Isle of Man Production TT. Tommy Robb (64) 2nd, Kevin Cass (65) 6th, almost blot out similarly-mounted Bill Smith, 1st

Above left
Historic day for the Bultaco marque. Ginger Molloy wins the 250 cc Ulster Grand Prix on his works TSS, 20 August 1966 – the factory's first ever classic victory

Left
Aussie Jack Findlay (250 Bultaco) at the East German GP, July 1966

important national 250 cc race on Easter Monday 1965 at Thruxton.

Tester Bruce Main-Smith concurred that 'as with the 125, the handling of which greatly impressed me, so with the 250 – there's a taut let's-crank-it-over-and-scratch quality to Bultaco navigation'. He found the 250 'extremely smooth' and 'would sing straight up to its peak of 9,200 rpm and give usable

power from 6,000 rpm upwards'. The brakes, clutch ('light and progressive'), and gearbox ('downward changes were good . . . upward . . . superlative') were also praised, and he summed up the bike in these terms: 'an easy machine to ride, and a rewarding one. It leaves the jockey free to think about the line, race tactics and the rest of the real business'.

As well as Ginger Molloy, two Britishers received factory support from Bultaco during 1965 – Ulsterman Tommy Robb, and London tuner Frank Sheene, whose son Barry was later to become a double world champion. Before long, a programme entry which read Sheene-Bultaco guaranteed that the race would see an ultra-quick and well-prepared motorcycle – a combination of bike and rider to be feared in the ranks of British short circuit racers during the sixties.

For anything below world class Grand Prix racing, the little Bultacos were still amongst the bikes to beat and were a familiar sight around the race paddocks of the world. In terms of racing success, 1966 had been one of Bultaco's best ever seasons, especially in the 250 class.

The Grand Prix results in the 250 included Jack

Findlay's 4th and Juan Blanco's 6th in the IoM TT, Tommy Robb's 6th in the Dutch, G Marsovski's 5th in Czechoslovakia, Findlay's 4th in Finland, a win for Ginger Molloy in Ulster (followed home by Marsovski and Kevin Cass), 4ths for Findlay in Italy and Japan, and a 6th in Japan for Tommy Robb. Jose Medrano had also taken a 6th in the 125 Spanish GP – the only points scored by the smaller machines – and Tommy Robb had actually gone up a capacity class and taken a 3rd in the 350 Ulster GP.

The year 1966 and Ulster had proved important for Bultaco on two counts. The first was Molloy's win – their first ever in a Grand Prix. The second was Tommy Robb's ride in the 350. Beaten only by Hailwood and Agostini, his exploits on a 252 cc TSS had shown Bultaco that competition in this class, which was dominated by ageing British singles, was less fierce than in the hotly-contested quarter-litre category. Like Aermacchi before them, Bultaco were soon to exploit this situation to their benefit.

Following Bultaco's entry into the off-road scene through Sammy Miller in the mid-1960's, production was concentrated upon this sector. This expansion continued apace in 1967, and soon the Barcelona factory could truly be said to be the market leader in this area.

In road racing, they were still essentially second-stringers, but the outstanding achievement of the year was the Isle of Man Diamond Jubilee TT Production race, in which Harry Lindsay, the importer for Southern Ireland, entered a team of three 250 Metralla Mk 2 sportsters ridden by Kevin Cass, Bill Smith, and Tommy Robb.

The talking point of the three-lap event was the shattering performance of the 250 class winner, Bill Smith, and second place man Robb, as they stormed around the $37\frac{3}{4}$ mile mountain circuit. The main interest centred on how it was possible for two road-going two-stroke singles to average 88.63 and 88.62 mph over perhaps the most arduous test of a racing motorcycle ever devised. In fact, it was a combination of several things – speed, reliability (even the third Metralla came in 6th), and superb handling and

Previous page
Oulton Park, 28 August 1967. In the 250 race Tommy Robb (Bultaco 2) leads Kent Andersson (Kawasaki 36) and Phil Read (Yamaha 38)

Right
Bultaco privateers Grant Gibson (42) and Martin Carney fight it out in the 250 cc race at Brands Hatch, 3 September 1967

brakes. The contribution of three excellent riders well versed in the circuit was the final clincher.

The Metrallas owed their speed in part to a racing kit which the factory brochure summed up thus: 'The kit can easily be installed by the customer himself and all that is required is a set of spanner, a medium-cut file, a drilling machine, three drills, and a dose of enthusiasm'. It cost US$389 and consisted of a tank, seat, bikini fairing, clip-ons, rearsets, cylinder barrel, head, and piston, expansion chamber exhaust, carburettor bellmouth, jets, cables, and even a racing spark plug.

In the 1967 Grands Prix, the TSS 125 took four 6ths: in the Spanish (J Medrano), French (J Vergenais), Ulster (Molloy), and Japanese (Barry Smith) races. Kevin Cass also took 5th in the Ulster. Grand Prix results for the 250s included Medrano's 3rd, Molloy's 4th and Robb's 5th in Spain; Findlay's 4th in West Germany, with Marsovski 5th and Schmid 6th; Molloy's 6th in the Dutch TT and Italian, and 5th in the Belgian and East German; G Marsovski's 6ths in East Germany, Ulster and Belgium, his 4th in Finland; and a 4th in Japan for Tommy Robb.

By 1968, Bultaco's full range consisted of 21 models — a far cry from the solitary Tralla 101 of a decade before — with capacities of 75, 100, 125, 175, 200, 250, and now 360 cc's. The latter was the fire-

Above

Prototype of 1968 type Bultaco 250 over-the-counter production racer seen at the 1967 French GP

Above right

In the race shop — works rider Ginger Molloy tries the riding position of the new racer in early 1968. Also in picture are Snr Bulto (in hat), Ing. Albeto Numen (glasses) and Paco Gonzalez

Right

Carney getting down to it with his smaller Bultaco, Mallory Park season opener, 3 March 1968

breathing 43.5 bhp unit of the El Bandido motocrosser, like much of the range, one of the new dirt bikes. But two of the total were updated versions of the TSS racers, with engine modifications, including restyled outer cases around the most important change of all — geared primary drive. Carburation was now by 32 mm Spanish Amal 389 B-32 GP, with 350 main jet on the 125 and 400 on the 250. Bultaco also took care of fitting electronic ignition to the 250 for the first time, and the maximum power was now 29 bhp at 11,500 rpm on the 125, and 38.8 bhp at 9,500 rpm on the 250.

Although these were relatively small changes, the engines were now housed in a totally revised chassis. The old 'plumber's nightmare' frame was replaced by a well proportioned twin-duplex construction akin to a miniature featherbed Manx. This carried a sleek, new fibre-glass tank and seat, but because of the Spanish government's insistence on Spanish-only components, the TSS was still delivered without a rev counter or proper racing tyres. When the first went on sale in Britain in May, prices had risen to £515 for the 125 and £525 for the 250.

By now, the factory's two leading riders were Ginger Molloy and Salvador Canellas. Despite the fact that their 125 cc machines were rapidly becoming outclassed at international level, they still managed

Right
A victorious Martin Carney with the victor's laurels, Good Friday meeting Brands Hatch, 12 April 1968

Below
Details of the 1968 250 TSS features included geared primary drive, water-cooling and six speeds. Cylinder head removed to show water jackets in barrel

Above
Barry Sheene began his racing career on Bultacos, here on a 350 TSS at Snetterton, 9 March 1969. His father Frank was a friend of Sr. Bulto

Below
Final version of the 'over-the-counter' Bultaco racers appeared in 1969. Water-cooling was still the simple thermo syphon method

to pull off some excellent results. Canellas, for example, scored Bultaco's second Grand Prix victory by winning the Spanish in front of a near hysterical home crowd, followed by Ginger Molloy in 2nd position. Canellas also finished 4th in the Dutch TT, as did Molloy in the Ulster, while Molloy pulled off a brilliant 2nd behind Phil Read's Yamaha in Holland. Tommy Robb, who had been 5th in Spain, made up for earlier retirements on Bultacos in the Isle of Man by coming home fourth.

One surprise of the 1968 Dutch TT was the appearance of a factory-prototype disc valve 125. Strangely enough, this was an air-cooled machine and was neither raced nor developed any further. Its design followed experiments carried out the previous year by Australian rider Kevin Cass, who converted his 125 Bultaco TSS engine to disc valve induction, and had also modified the top end with various Suzuki and Yamaha components.

In the 250 class, Molloy was the leading Bultaco rider, with a 2nd in West Germany, 3rd in Spain, 5th in East Germany, 6th in Czechoslovakia, and 4ths in Finland and Ulster, to finish 5th overall in the championships. He also had some excellent rides on a prototype of a new TSS 350, which showed that Bultaco had taken the lesson of the previous year's Ulster to heart. On this machine he came 2nd in the Dutch TT and 4th in both West and East Germany.

Club rider Chris McGahan on his 350 Bultaco TSS in the early 1970s. By then the Spanish single was totally outclassed by the latest Yamaha twins on all but the tightest and shortest circuits

But by the time the TSS 350 went into production at the end of 1968, the machine was at least a couple of years too late. It used the engine from the 360 motocrosser, with the bore decreased to 83.2 mm and the same stroke at 64 mm, enabling it to achieve the qualifying capacity with 347.95 cc. With a 10:1 compression ratio, the air-cooled unit gave 47.5 bhp at 8,500 rpm. Recognising the problems they had experienced with the B-32 GP carburettor on the smaller bikes, Bultaco opted for a 38 mm Amal Concentric Mk 1, and the gearbox was a five-speeder, with a new geared primary drive.

Another deviation from the smaller engine's design was the 350's oval twin-plug combustion chamber. The factory specification sheet shows the Femsa ignition firing both plugs at once, and Bultaco actually listed a Lodge RL5l for the front and a shorter RL49 for the rear plug. In practice, only one plug was used, with many riders following Frank Sheene's lead by using the single plug conversion. Unhappy with the standard combustion chamber shape Sheene filled the existing oval with alloy weld. He then re-machined the head so that it ended up looking like the 125/250, and finally retapped the plug hole vertically and the central to the rear-offset combustion chamber.

The all-alloy 350 unit was an exceedingly simple design, and even though it was in many ways just a larger version of Bultaco's basic design concept, there were some fundamental differences, like the geared primary drive. Although this had been used before on the 125 and TSS 250 to replace the unreliable chain drive, the version on these bikes actually ran the other way round. To maintain clockwise clutch rotation on the smaller models, the factory had been forced to add an idle gear between the clutch and crankshaft. There was also an outrigger bearing outside the magneto flywheel to control crankshaft whip, but this occasionally had the effect of snapping the crankshaft off flush with the outside of the flywheel. What with bearing failures and crankshaft breakages, the new system had proved almost as unreliable as the chain it replaced, so as a result there were a host of dissatisfied Bultaco owners around in 1968 and 1969.

An effective cure would have been to remove the outrigger bearing altogether. Despite allowing a certain amount of whip, this gets rid of the problems with the bearing and crankshaft breakage. But on the larger engine, Bultaco thought they would eliminate the problem entirely by allowing the clutch to rotate anti-clockwise, as with most geared primary drives.

Unfortunately, they were still plagued with primary drive problems on the 350, as the nut retaining the drive pinion on the end of the crankshaft had the habit of working loose and breaking its split pin in the process – finally boring a neat hole straight through the outer primary drive cover.

The 350 was not to be granted the time to taste success as its smaller brothers had, but even so, a young rider soon to make his mark in the world began racing during 1968 on a Bultaco – Barry Sheene, son of ace tuner Frank. By 1969, Sheene had become a full works Bultaco rider, winning events throughout Britain; but the writing was on the wall

Bultaco made a return to road racing in 1976 with new 50 and 125 Grand Prix racers. The smaller mount is shown. This is Angel Nieto's machine, world champion for Bultaco in 1976 and 1977

for the TSS range, with the advent of the vastly superior Yamaha production racers such as the TD2 and TR2. Like all the other production singles, the Bultacos just couldn't live with these superfast Japanese twins.

As a result, all three TSS models were dropped from production at the end of 1969, except for a few machines used exclusively for the Spanish national championship. This followed a disappointing Grand Prix season, in which few Bultaco points had been scored and Molloy was the only consistent rider. Even he had only gained points in the 125 and 350 classes, with not a single point gained in the 250 races all year. One high point to restore Bultaco's self-esteem, however, was that the Barcelona 24 Hours endurance race was won by a 360 cc 'prototype'.

Into the 1970s, and the factory had streamlined its production to concentrate almost entirely on off-road machines, with no road racers and only a few roadsters. This was to be the pattern of Bultaco production for the next few years, until the introduction of new roadsters in the late 1970s. But despite deleting the racers from their catalogue, Bultaco found it hard to stay away from tarmac sport and remained ardent contenders in the annual Barcelona 24 Hours race.

For the 1972 event, held on 8/9 July, the factory

entered Benjamin Grau and Juan Bordens on the very same 360 cc machine which had won back in 1969. Classed as a prototype, it used a modified motocross engine mounted in a road racing frame and sported an expansion chamber exhaust, twin headlamps, a large-capacity tank, and a massive 240 mm four leading shoe front drum brake. The combination of two skilled riders and the powerful, light, sweet-handling Bultaco proved unbeatable that year, coming out the overall victors as well as class winners, and setting a new record in the process.

Although they could not repeat the win in the 1973 race, this was even more memorable, for Bultaco entered only the one 360cc machine, this time entrusting it to the completely amateur team of Jaime Alguersuari, a well-known Spanish photographer and journalist, and Enrique de Juan. Despite being an unknown quantity, this pairing proved to be a good choice, with the yellow Bultaco surprising even the most ardent of the marque's supporters by not only completing the 24 Hours, but finishing 2nd with 704 laps completed, behind winners Canellas and Grau on the works 860 Ducati and ahead of an impressive array of mega-bikes. These included the 3rd place team of Godier/Genoud on one of the very successful Egli-Hondas. Just to round off the factory's day, a Bultaco ridden by Collado and Marsinac won the hotly contested 250 class.

Everyone thought these Barcelona *24 Horas* (24 Hours) victories were to be the company's racing swansong. But in 1976 Bultaco returned – and with a full Grand Prix challenge no less.

This all stemmed from a meeting which Spanish World Champion Angel Nieto had with the Dutch engineers, Jan Thiel and Martin Mijwaart, the men behind the Jamathi and Piovaticci two-stroke racers. At the 1975 Finnish GP, Nieto asked Thiel and Mijwaart if they wanted to work in Spain building bikes for him. As the Italian Piovaticci team from Pesaro was being forced out of racing at the end of the year due to financial difficulties, both were keen on the idea. The result was a contract between the Spanish Motorcycle Federation, Bultaco and the two Dutch designers, with Nieto riding the bikes.

The 1976 plan hinged on being able to contest all the 50 and 125 world championship rounds. Because there was so little time left in which to develop brand new machines, it was crucial that the 50 and 125 bikes the Dutchmen had designed and built for the Piovaticci team were obtained. At first, there were problems, for although Egidio Piovaticci the owner of the machines was hard-hit financially, he was none too keen to sell until eventually forced to.

Following Nieto's success, Ricardo Tormo (shown here) won the 50 cc world title in 1978 and 1981 on Bultaco machinery

After much trouble, the machines and parts arrived in Spain, only to be greeted with a fresh set of problems in the shape of a lengthy strike at the Bultaco factory. This, Bultaco's first industrial trouble, was only a foretaste of what was to come in the way of unrest at the Barcelona plant. Even so, many people at Bultaco, especially team manager Cesar Rojo, worked long hours in their determination to get the new racing team off the ground.

Eventually, the new road racing department was ready, but plans for a completely new 125 had to be shelved – simply because of lack of time. So Bultaco's 1976 season commenced with the 'old' Piovaticci machinery, tuned and updated, together with a new paint job and Bultaco's logos on their tanks.

There was one complete 50 with two engines, and one complete 125 – not much to start a season, even though Bultaco completed a second monocoque frame for the second 50 during the season. But in a fairy-tale comeback by the end of racing that year Bultaco and the two Dutchmen had won their first world title, the 50 cc, after the victorious Nieto had stormed home 1st in the Italian, Dutch, Swedish, West German and Spanish GPs. Add to this a 3rd in Yugoslavia, and a 2nd in Belgium and the championship was won with ease.

Not so for the 125. The Belgian GP was Nieto's only victory, and the title went to Morbidelli-mounted Italian Pier-Paulo Bianchi. Quite simply, the 125 twin was neither reliable nor quick enough to win the title. Even so, the 1976 results were good for Bultaco, with the 50 cc world championship and manufacturer's award, second spot in the 125 cc class, and both 50 and 125 Spanish national titles.

The 1976 works racers were known as the TSS Mk2. The 50 cc (49.76 cc) was a single cylinder disc valve engine with bore and stroke of 40 x 39.6 mm. The power output was 17 bhp at 16,000 rpm, and there was a 28 mm Mikuni carburettor, 'home-made' electronic ignition, plus a six-speed gearbox, dry clutch and geared primary drive. The engine was water-cooled with forced circulation by a Bosch electric pump to an aluminium radiator on the nose of

Enrique de Juan (360 Bultaco) who, together with co-rider Jaime Alguersuari, was a runner-up in the 1973 Barcelona 24 hours, behind the works 860 Ducati of Cannellas and Grau.

the fairing. The frame was of monocoque construction in stainless steel, and there was a 1.5 gallon tank. Rear suspension was by twin Koni shock absorbers and the wheels were five-spoke cast-alloy Campagnolos with single Scarab discs and Brembo calipers front and rear. Dry, the machine weighed a mere 57 kg (126 lb).

The 125 was a 43 x 43 mm disc valve twin, giving 39 bhp at 14,500 rpm. Twin 28 mm Mikunis were used and ignition was a Krober electronic system. Primary drive was provided by gears off the middle of the crankshaft to a dry clutch and six-speed gearbox. The cycle parts were to similar specifications as the smaller machines, but the tank capacity was 3.3 gallons and there were twin front disc brakes. The larger machine tipped the scales at 87 kg (192 lb) dry.

During the closed season, Nieto publicly stated that he did not wish to contest the 50 class in 1977. *Motor Cycle News* ran the story in October 1976 under the dramatic headline: 'Why I quit the tiddlers'. In fact, Nieto wanted to concentrate on winning the 125 title and developing a 250 for 1978.

Things never worked out like this, and when the new season arrived, Nieto was out again on both the 50 and the 125, while the promised 250 never materialised on the race circuit. For 1977, Nieto was joined by fellow Spaniard Ricardo Tormo, and at the second round of the 50 cc championships, the Italian GP at Imola, a new tiddler appeared.

Barcelona 1973; pit stop after de Juan had crashed after 22 hours – the 360 Bultaco still managed to finish 2nd overall, a magnificent achievement

The new racer made extensive use of magnesium to bring the weight down to 55 kg (121 lb), the bare minimum for the class. The design included crankcases which were cast in one piece. Detailed modifications included new disc brakes, an aluminium clutch, and Motoplat electronic ignition.

Backed up by Tormo's sterling efforts, Nieto took the world 50 cc title for the sixth time, with wins in the Spanish, Yugoslavian and Dutch rounds. Tormo had his first ever Grand Prix win at the final race of the season, the Swedish, where on the Anderstorp circuit he squarely beat all the leading contenders, Nieto included. In the 125 class, Bianchi and the Morbidelli again thwarted Nieto's challenge, even though he won the opening bout in Venezuela, as well as the Dutch and Swedish rounds.

But Nieto was becoming increasingly unsettled in the Bultaco race team. Matters were to come to a head the next year when his performances deteriorated. After a poor 7th place in the 125 race in the opening round at Mugello, he joined the rival Minarelli team, and came within a whisker of winning the world title for the Italian factory, just being pipped by early runner Eugenio Lazzarini on an MBA. The two would later become team mates in the all-conquering Garelli GP team in the early eighties.

Meanwhile, Bultaco had found another champion in Ricardo Tormo, who won all the 50 cc rounds in 1978 bar two, and in the process became the new world champion and made it three in a row for the Barcelona factory.

The following year saw Tormo repeating the error made by Nieto in attempting to win the 125 title at the expense of the 50 cc class. Although he won at the Finnish and gained two 2nds, these were his only finishes on the Bultaco twin; while his defence of the 50 cc title was almost non-existent, with a 5th in Yugoslavia being the best he could achieve.

Tormo was out of the Grand Prix scene for the whole of 1980; but in 1981, he won Bultaco's fourth and final world title, after victories in Italy, Spain, Yugoslavia, Holland, Belgium and the San Marino GP at Imola. The Spaniard was backed up by Dutch rider, Theo Timmer, who won the final round at Brno, Czechoslovakia. Bultaco had learned their lesson well. They did not even bother to contest the 125 class!

In fact, behind this outward promise, the factory had almost reached the end of the road. Despite the racing success and numerous achievements gained by their dirt bikes world wide, a series of strikes had crippled Bultaco to the point where it could no longer meet its wages bill. Left-wing elements within

the 465-strong workforce had put the knife into the company to such an extent that Bultaco's founder, Francisco Bulto, was even barred from entering the factory which he had nurtured. Feelings within the workforce ran so high that an effigy of Sr. Bulto was actually publicly displayed with a rope around its neck and then burned outside the factory gates.

The factory officially closed on 22 December 1979. It was reopened (without the Bulto family) in May 1980 with Juan Chalamanch in charge and with only 200 of its former staff. Formerly Sr. Bulto's deputy, Chalamanch took over the Bulto presidency following a cash injection by the Spanish government of 80 million pesetas (about £3,077,000).

Although this allowed the factory to begin limited production again, things were not as they had been before the period of industrial unrest, and much bitterness remained. In any case, the continued elements of labour troubles, a depressed market for off-road machines, greatly increased Japanese competition and the opening up of the domestic market combined effectively to kill what had become the most prestigious of Spain's motorcycle companies.

By 1983, the marque whose thumbs-up logo had typified so much of its progress since its farmyard conception in 1958 was almost no more, with factory and workforce awaiting a government scheme called *Plan de Reconversion*. This called for all the Catalan factories with financial troubles (Bultaco-Montesa-Ossa) to join as one. Conceived by the unions with official backing, the idea was for Montesa to take over both its erstwhile rivals in one new company. But the scheme was never really a starter. The ultimate result was the death of Spain's most famous racing marque shortly afterwards.

Derbi

A dream came true when the diminutive Angel Nieto became Spain's first motorcycle world champion and thrust Derbi into the road racing limelight a quarter of a century ago. Nieto's 1969 win was a fitting vindication for Derbi, for whilst other Spanish makers had switched their attention to trials and motocross, Derbi stuck to Grand Prix racing to try to boost sales of its humble road models. But their policy paid off handsomely and within four years, Nieto and Derbi won five world titles in the 'classic' era.

But who are Derbi? The name is an acronym for DERivados de BIcicletas (derivative of bicycles). In 1922, Simeon Rabasa Singla had opened a small workshop for the repair and hire of pedal cycles. The location was in the village of Mollet, some 12 miles from Barcelona, and from these humble beginnings

was to emerge what has since become Spain's strongest and most successful motorcycle manufacturer.

No one would have predicted this in the early days, for then the company seemed soundly established in the cycle business. However, with the formation of a limited liability company under the name Bicicletus Rabasa on 5 May 1944, Singla had moved into the manufacturing business, a step which heralded a period of intense activity for the new company. As a result, by 1949 Bicicletus Rabasa had become one of Spain's major producers of pedal cycles.

However pedal cycles were not to remain the firm's sole product for long, and as early as 1946 work had begun on a powered version. In 1949, supported by the success of the thriving bicycle business, this was launched under the name SRS (the founder's initials).

Although the SRS used what was essentially a conventional pedal cycle chassis, this featured several noteworthy additions besides its 48 cc engine. These included plunger rear suspensions, a sprung saddle, a motorcycle-type fuel tank and a motorcycle exhaust system. The latter was very elaborate for this type of machine, comprising a single rearward-facing exhaust pipe (the cylinder head was reversed) which ran into a branch pipe from which two separate silencers ran back, one on either side of the frame, directly level with the cylinder barrel. As the engine was mounted very high in the frame, the effect was a true 'high level' exhaust system.

The power unit was a simple pistón port two-stroke, with two speeds and hand operated gearchange! The engine produced 1.5 bhp at 4,500 rpm on a compression ratio of 5.5:1, which was sufficient to propel the machine to a maximum speed of 27 mph, but was hardly enough to set the pulse racing or even give a hint of the victorious Grand Prix racers for which the factory was later to become famous.

Despite its humble pretensions the SRS proved to be very successful, which pointed the way forward and instigated a major change in company direction and policy. As a result, the firm's name was changed on 7 November 1950, now becoming the Nacional Motor SA, and production was devoted almost exclusively to motorcycle manufacture.

The Barcelona Trades Fair that year had already witnessed the company's first real motorcycle. This was a bulbous twin port single cylinder engine of

The first Derbi star was Jose Busquets, seen here during the 50 cc French Grand, 13 May 1962

Jawa design, which gave 9 bhp at 4,000 rpm and drove through a four-speed gearbox with footchange. This was followed with a varity of two-strokes including a twin cylinder 350 which again showed much Czech influence. But with Spanish economics dictating a trend towards smaller engines, Derbi eventually shelved the 250 and 350 models at the end of the 1950's, in favour of a 95 cc unit. Further development produced an even more efficient 74 cc motor. It was followed by a 65 cc version. Finally the firm settled on 49 cc capacity.

By the time (1960) Derbi had begun to enter local racing events, but Jose Busquets, the first Derbi works rider, had no luck. He managed to put up several good performances but, whenever victory was in sight, his bike broke down.

Enter Francisco Tombas who had joined Derbi as a 23 year old mechanic back in 1953. Tombas had previously designed and raced several home-built 100 cc prototypes and in the process not only proved just about unbeatable in his class around the twists and turns of Montjuich Park, Barcelona, but also established his worth as a skilled designer and tuner. His bikes were fast and they were also reliable, just what Derbi needed. Drafted into the race team his ability was soon a major influence.

Promoted to race chief in late 1960, Tombas produced the firm's first successful 50 cc racer, winning a three hour race at Castellon with a five-speed gearbox, 20 mm Del'Orto SS racing carb and 9 bhp. A year later Tombas designed Derbi's first disc valve unit. This had eight speeds, a 24 mm carb and give 11.5 bhp at 12,000 rpm. By 1962 with modified porting and exhaust the power was up to 12.5 bhp at 13,000 rpm: Derbi were now ready for serious action.

The first foray onto the world stage came that year, with the introduction by the FIM of a 50 cc category into the world road racing championships. Fortuitously, the very first round was to be the 1962 Spanish Grand Prix, held at Barcelona in May. Derbi's sole entrant in the race was Busquets, whose opposition included the likes of Anscheidt, Taveri and Robb on an array of micro racers from around the world including Kreidler, Honda and Suzuki. The result of this seemingly unequal contest amazed everyone, with the Derbi rider finishing a close second to Anscheidt's number one Kreidler, and in the process hounding him all the way to the finish line.

Although Derbi did not contest any further world championship rounds that year, the factory nevertheless had the satisfaction of winning both the Spanish and French national championships for the

class. Until the end of 1964 the works Derbi team raced almost exclusively at home, with only limited participation in the Grands Prix. But in 1965 a water-cooled machine made its debut. It gave 14.5 bhp at 14,000 rpm and was more powerful than the Suzuki twins of the period; but ultimately, Japanese quality beat Spanish metallurgy.

Australian Barry Smith gave Derbi their first classic victory at the 1968 Austrian GP (a non-championship event). And, with FIM restrictions dictating a single cylinder and six speeds for the 50 cc class from 1969, Smith went on to score the company's first IoM TT victory, and finished the season in third place in the championship. Team mate Angel Nieto was fourth.

Realising that they had a real chance of success under the new FIM formula, which stipulated single-cylinder engines and a maximum of six gear ratios, Derbi built a completely new bike for 1969. However, in the early races they were outpaced by the Dutch based Van Veen Kreidler team, and it was not until the Dutch TT at the end of June that the Spanish bikes were really competitive.

There, Nieto led until big-end failure put him out. Team mate Barry Smith went on to win. Smith won a week later in Belgium, with Nieto grabbing victory the following week at the Sachsenring, East Germany. A second success, in Ulster, put him well on

Customer racer, the 1965 Derbi Carreras Cliente;
12 bhp and five speeds ensured its owner a genuinely
competitive ride

the way to the championship, although it was not until the final round, in Yugoslavia, that he got ahead of Aalt Toersen (Kreidler) for the title.

Born on 25 January 1947, Nieto started racing at the age of thirteen. That was in 1960, when he rode a well used 50 cc Derbi in a junior event at Grenada. Because there was no tiddler class he was forced to compete with 125s, but even so finished third. Then came several years of racing largely uncompetitive bikes after a spell in the Bultaco race shop as a mechanic. In 1965 he joined the Mototrans factory which made Ducatis under licence, but it was not a happy year. By then the four-stroke singles were no match for the ever-improving Bultaco and Montesa two-strokes; Mototrans and Nieto parted company mid-season. Nieto's big chance came when he joined the Derbi works team for 1967; he responded in fine style by winning the Spanish championship, before getting into Grand Prix action the following year. When he returned to Spain after clinching the 1969 50 cc world championship Angel was escorted, bull-fighter fashion, through the streets of Barcelona.

Overnight he became a national hero; the success of *el Nino* (the Boy) was the first world title win by a

Spaniard in the history of road racing, and for Nieto it was a dream come true – a dream that began when he was a youngster doing odd jobs in a Madrid motorcycle shop years earlier.

Angel Nieto retired in the early 1980s after 13 world titles and winning countless GPs. Except for Giacomo Agostini he was the most successful motorcycle racer of all time.

Back at the Derbi factory in Mollet, race chief Tombas had not rested on his laurels. Why not a 125 cc twin? So in 1967 he had constructed an 'unofficial' prototype – a narrow angle V-twin! Basically the larger engine had two superimposed cylinders with a very narrow inclined angle between them. The cylinders were set horizontally to lower the centre of gravity and to assist cooling. The engine, like the 50 of the period, was of disc valve design, with the twin rotary disc valve situated on the left hand side of the crankcases. Initially the air-cooled engine produced 30 bhp, which by its final season had been upped to 32 bhp. The power was directed through an eight-speed gearbox.

Although technically fascinating, the V-twin never achieved the success of the later Derbi 125, or,

Above
Australian Barry Smith gave Derbi their first Grand Prix victory, the 1968 Isle of Man 50 cc TT

Below
Technically interesting, but a flop results-wise, the Derbi 125 cc v-twin first appeared in 1967

Above
Derbi GP v-twin, Hutchinson 100, 10 August 1969

Right
A plug change for Derbi star Angel Nieto, Belgian GP, 6 July 1969

Above far right
The Derbi squad warm up for an international 50 cc race in Spain, circa 1969

Far right
The 1970 works Derbi 50 cc Grand Prix racer exudes speed and style in every line

Above
Derbi's number one, Angel Nieto, circa 1971

Right
Angel Nieto, nicknamed el nino *(the boy) was the first Spanish rider to win a world championship. This photograph was taken at the 1970 Ulster GP*

Above far right
The 1972 50 cc world championship series was the closest in history – the two duellists were Nieto Derbi (2) and the Dutchman De Vries on a Kreidler. Nieto took the verdict after the 5 round contest by the smallest of margins, the final result being decided on the riders' top race times

Far right
Nieto was a double world champion in 1972 (50 and 125 cc). He is shown here on the larger model winning at Imola. At the end of the year Derbi retired from GP racing and the Spanish star signed for the Italian Morbidelli team

for that matter, the smaller bikes which the factory raced at the same time. The bike's only placing in the top six of a world championship was a fourth gained by the Frenchman Roca in the 1969 French GP at Le Mans.

For 1970, Derbi made the decision to drop the V-twin and concentrate on building a totally new bike to contest the 50 cc category with a reduced squad of three riders – Nieto, Canallas and Bordens. This strategy was completely vindicated when Nieto won the first four GPs in succession and romped home champion for the second year.

The real excitement in the Derbi camp, however, was a new 125. Francisco Tombas had been far from happy with the earlier V-twin. His new baby was a totally new water-cooled parallel twin, with a capacity of 123.96 cc (43.40 x 41.90 mm). With six speeds it pumped out an impressive 34 bhp at 14,500 rpm.

Introduced halfway through the season, the newcomer proved a winner first time out, with Nieto aboard, at the high speed Belgian Spa circuit. This was followed by further maximum points scores in East Germany, Italy and Spain to give Derbi second place in the world championships, confirming the factory's clear intention of joining battle for the world title the following year.

But 1971 didn't turn out quite as Derbi had planned, even though during the close season Tombas had extracted more power from both the 50 and 125 engines. Although the Spanish combination of Nieto and Derbi tasted glory in the larger class, the tiddlers proved a different matter, with the Van Veen Kreidler team doing everything in their power to win. This included using a whole host of riding talent, including even Barry Sheene and Jarno Saarinen. Eventually Kreidler took the title, won by the Dutchman Jan DeVries.

Derbi then spent most of the winter of 1971–2 making absolutely sure that the next season's results would come easier. Much detail work boosted the 125's power output to 40 bhp at 15,500 rpm, giving a claimed 145 mph on the fastest circuits. With the smaller unit power was upped to 18 bhp and over 120 mph. The hard work throughout the winter proved worthwhile with Nieto and Derbi claiming both titles.

At the end of the 1972 season Derbi retired from serious GP racing – the official reason being to concentrate on a new series of production roadsters. However, this was not to mean a complete exit as is usually the case, for various tarmac racers appeared afterwards, including a works 250 twin and 50/125 production bikes. The 247 cc twin was a pukka works, no-cost-spared effort producing 58 bhp. This had first appeared at the 1971 Austrian GP in the hands of Nieto and Sheene.

However, it was not until 1972 that it achieved anything of note, including a victory by the Swedish

In 1973 Derbi produced a batch of Angel Nieto replicas. Unfortunately they were not the real thing, short of both power and reliability

The 1980 version of the water-cooled 125 racing twin, sadly only seen in its homeland

rider Borje Jansson at the Austrian GP. This was sadly to be a victim of the 1972 cutback, and was never raced outside Spain again, despite scoring an unprecedented run of success in the Spanish national championships between 1971 and 1980 in the hands of Grau and Nieto.

The year 1972 was the end of an era in another sense, for it marked the fiftieth anniversary of the founding of the original Rabasa workshop. Its successor, Derbi, now embraced the three villages of Mollet, Martorelles and San Fausto, employing over 600 staff. Quite some progress! An echo of the racing successes scored by the factory was evident with the release in 1973 of a single batch of fifty Angel Nieto 'Replica' 50 cc – 48.77 cc (38 x 43 mm) – racers. However, although *looking* the part, their performance and reliability left much to be desired. A 125 production racer was also built. Like the 50, the 125 twin was air-cooled, with six speeds. However, it was a much better machine as I was able to sample first hand during one of my visits to the factory in

November 1975. Maximum speed was over 130 mph, with vivid acceleration, thanks in no small part to its lightness and compact design. Braking was by twin Scarab discs at the front and a drum at the rear. Front forks were Marzocchi, with 30 mm stanchions. My test session lasted approximately 30 minutes and to underline the power of Derbi in their own locality is to recall that certain roads were closed especially for this test session! Unlike the smaller bike, the 125 never entered production, although at the time there were plans to race at least one in Britain, with myself as team manager. The most likely rider would have been 125 expert Clive Horton, with whom I had talks, amongst other leading lightweight jockeys.

And so to the mid 1980's, a decade on, and once more Derbi proved that they had lost none of their expertise for making 'strokers fly, even at the highest level, when they gained both the 80 and 125 cc world titles.

Lube

This marque is one of Spain's oldest manufacturers. For many years they were closely connected with NSU of West Germany. Luis Bojarano, the head of

Far left
Brands Hatch 14 October 1962, Mike O'Rourke and the 125 Lube two-stroke single, designed with the help of Hermann Meier

Below far left
Lube engine with steeply inclined Amal carb, sandcast crankcase assembly, air-cooled cylinder and cut-off expansion box

Left
Unusual leading link forks, external dampers and cutaway front brake plate of the 1962 124 cc Lube racer

Below
Air-cooled Lube 247 cc piston port twin which made its debut in 1965, but was largely unsuccessful

Lube, built NSU-powered two and four-stroke road-sters using his own frames with engines ranging from 49 to 247 cc. The factory also made its own racers: at first a 125 single, later a 250 twin; both were piston port two-strokes.

The well known engine tuner Hermann Meier had a spell with the factory in 1962 and 1963 before joining Royal Enfield in England, where he was responsible for developing the GP5 two-fifty racer (see *Classic British Racing Motorcycles* Osprey Publishing).

The 1962 125 Lube had a 124 cc (56 x 54 mm) engine with piston port induction and full unit construction, which with a compression ratio of 10:1 from its German Mahle piston produced around 18 bhp. Carburation was either via a Dell'Orto SSI or Amal GP carburettor, with remote float chamber. In October 1962 it was extensively tested in Britain by Mike O'Rourke who had previously ridden a Meier-tuned Ariel Arrow to 7th place in the 1960 Isle of Man Lightweight TT. O'Rourke rode the Lube at Brands Hatch in a couple of races, but ultimately decided to stick with his own Bultaco TSS production racer and the Lube was returned to Spain.

The machine had made its race debut earlier that year in the Spanish GP at Montjuich Park, Barcelona, where it proved no match for the latest works bikes from Japan and Italy.

In 1963 a new engine was designed and built; this featured a disc inlet valve driven from the nearside end of the crankshaft, three transfer ports and water-cooling. A front exhaust port was used, so that the water inlets were positioned either side of it

and the exit was from the rear of the cylinder head which was also liquid-cooled.

After the departure of Hermann Meier, development slowed and in fact the bike only made one classic appearance. This was the Czechoslovakian GP where the German rider Sauter finished way down the field in 18th position.

Lube's final racing design was a 250 cc two-stroke twin. It was air-cooled with large areas of finning on both the cylinder barrels and heads, a dry clutch, steeply angled carburettors and five speeds. It made several appearances in 1965, including the Spanish Grand Prix, but again performance was not on par with the latest factory bikes and the whole project was soon abandoned.

Montesa

As outlined at the start of this chapter it was the partnership of Pedro Permanyer and Francisco Bulto that was responsible for not only founding the Montesa concern, but also the birth of the Spanish motorcycle industry itself.

After many months of research and development by Bulto, the designer, and Permanyer, in charge of production, the pair saw the first fruits of their hard work finally pay off with a bike which they entered in the Race of Regularity, organised by the *Real Moto Club de Cataluna*, and held in February 1945. This

The 1948 Dutch TT saw the first appearance outside Spain of a racing Montesa. This was followed up in 1949 by the greatly improved X49 model, the first Montesa to sport telescopic front forks

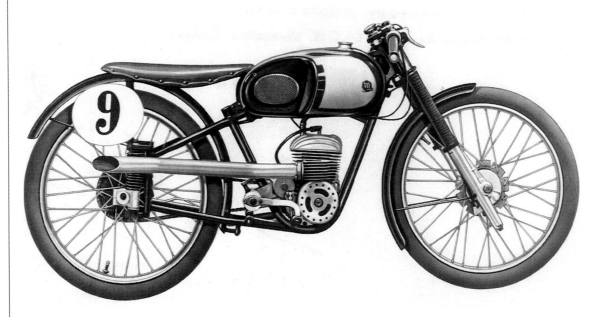

prototype, referred to simply as the model XX was a simple single cylinder piston port two-stroke of 98 cc (45.6 x 60 mm), with twin exhaust ports. It featured a hand operated three-speed gearbox, and an unsprung frame with blade-type forks using a single centre spring.

The production model of this machine was first shown to the Spanish public at the Official Samples fair held in Barcelona in June 1945, and was greeted enthusiastically.

In August of that year, five members of the production team, each riding one of the new machines, successfully completed the trip to the Balneary region of Caldas de Bohi, in the central Pyranees. Even today this area still poses a challenge to the motorcyclist, but the Montesa men undertook the journey at a time before any roads were constructed in the locality; as a result, the intrepid team had to negotiate everything from rock-strewn fords to craggy mountain tops. When they reached their destination, they discovered that they were pioneers in the truest sense, as no vehicle – with either two or four wheels – had previously succeeded in reaching Balneary. The event was widely publicised throughout Spain, and did much to establish Montesa in the public eye, so that from then on the name Montesa became almost synonymous with 'motorcycle'.

Later that year, and another first: half a dozen Montesas were in the entry for the inaugural race meeting that November over the new Montjuich Park circuit in Barcelona. In their category, the 100 cc class, Montesa gained the first five places – the first of a number of victories which the marque had while they made this engine.

By the end of 1945, two new models had appeared. One was a special 'ladies' version of the original machine; while the other, more significantly, was a larger 124.9 cc (51.50 x 60 mm) machine. In 1946 Montesa not only won the 100 cc Spanish national road racing championship, but also took the 125 category.

The following year the partners Bulto and Permanyer, as designer and manufacturer respectively, formed an official company – Permanyer SA de Industrias Mecanicas – with its headquarters at Calle Corcega 480, Barcelona, and with Montesa as its brand name.

A milestone in the fledgling company's history came in 1948, when a trio of Montesa 125 racers competed abroad successfully for the first time. At the Dutch TT, in June, their results of 5th, 9th and 15th among the world's finest were outstanding achievements.

J S Bulto (left) and J De Ortueta on 124 Montesas, Isle of Man TT, June 1951

Roadster production continued apace up to this time, although the 98 cc designs had been discontinued to allow the manufacturing facilities to concentrate exclusively on the 125. This was not due to any particular shortcomings of the smaller machines, simply that the 125 was becoming one of the most popular models throughout the country, and Montesa's output capacity was limited at this time. More sporting success and even more demand for its production machines resulted in a move on 19 June 1950, to new works at Calle Pamplona, also in Barcelona.

The expansion in business meant that an increase in the sporting budget could be allowed in 1951 for road racing and long distance trials. The Spanish GP that year, held on 8 April at Barcelona's Montjuich Park, was a full Grand Prix counting towards the world championship and Montesa were amongst the 27 entrants. The riders J S Bulto (a relation of the designer) and A Elizade scored fifth and sixth places. But even better was to come. Spurred on by this success Montesa sent a team to take part in the Isle of

Man Tourist Trophy races, then the premier event in the world. To the amazement of the pundits, the Spanish marque repeated its Spanish GP results, with 5th and 6th places in the Ultra Lightweight TT. Bulto and Jose Liobet the riders, averaged 63.46 mph and 61.18 mph respectively for the two lap, 75.5 mile race. The same month, the Barcelona Samples Fair was again the venue for the launch of a new Montesa roadster, when the 125 cc D-51 was announced.

For the first time on a production Montesa, this used telescopic front forks and plunger rear suspension – both appearing first on the 125 X49 racer in 1949. Unusually, the forks had lower legs which extended several inches below the front wheel spindle, which was carried by lugs cast on to the front of the sliders. This design was to remain a feature of the marque for many years and was later adopted by several other manufacturers for their off-road models.

In September 1951, Montesa took part for the first time in the ISDT, staged that year around the town of Varese in northern Italy. The factory entered two riders – G Cavestany and F Bulto – the latter none

One of the 1951 Montesas, featuring several modifications from earlier examples, including a redesigned engine

other than the chief designer and part owner of the firm. After surviving the rigours of six long days of competition covering in excess of 2000 kilometres, the pair emerged unscathed with a bronze medal apiece.

By 1952, Montesa had largely withdrawn from sport to concentrate on production and design of new roadsters. This resulted in the Brio 90 being introduced – a tuned version of the D-51 which it superseded. This was displayed for the first time at the 1953 Swiss motorcycle show in Geneva. The Brio 90 was the factory's first attempt at export and the model proved a winner, not only with the buying public, but by taking a host of trophies in sporting trials and rallies and minor racing events.

The Brio 80 appeared in 1954. This not only gave more torque and power, but was also the first Montesa aimed at serious pillion work – even though it retained its 125 cc capacity and three-speed gearbox.

Also in this year Montesa returned to the Isle of Man, where the latest racer, now called the Sprint, made its debut. Its production-based single cylinder piston port engine produced in the region of 14 bhp, giving a 90 mph speed potential. This enabled works rider Johnny Grace to gain seventh place against all the top teams of the day, including MV and Mondial. Later the same combination of machine and rider finished eighth at the Ulster GP.

Encouraged by this, designer Bulto increased his endeavours to perfect the racing effort. The result was a new version based on the Sprint. Outwardly, the machine's most noticeable feature was a full fairing. In fact the Montesa was one of the very first motorcycles anywhere in the world to employ streamlining which was constructed in plastic. Other changes saw the weight reduced to a mere 55 kg (121 lb) and with further tuning measures, maximum speed was in excess of 95 mph – high for the time. The new racer's debut under fire came at the Spanish GP, the last meeting of the 1954 classic calendar. In finishing third and fourth Montesa's streamlined machines gave the Barcelona factory their best inter-

Montesa returned to the Isle of Man for the 1954 TT, and in the Ultra Lightweight (125) event one of the new Sprint models ridden by Johnny Grace finished 7th against all the top works teams of the day

national performance to date, with only race winner Provini (Mondial) and Columbo (MV) ahead of them. However, it should be noted that none of the NSU's works team were present, withdrawn following the death of the 1954 125 cc World Champion, Austrian Ruppert Hollaus, killed during practice for the Italian GP at Monza the previous month.

But perhaps the biggest surprise that year was the decision to display the whole range of Montesa's roadsters at London's Earls Court Show in November. This was a bold and calculated move – one intended to foster international recognition and so increase sales. The policy worked, with several European countries signing up at the show to become Montesa importers.

By 1955, sales had grown to record levels – so much so that it was necessary to move the administration offices from the plant to make more room for production facilities to meet the increased demand for the company's most popular models, the Brio 90 and Brio 80.

With the 90's comfortable practicality and the 80's more sporting performance, Montesa easily led the Spanish motorcycle production league table. By the mid-1950's the domestic market had seen many others attempt to emulate Montesa's success. But very few actually managed it – most expiring as quickly as they had appeared.

The improved Brio 91 was launched in 1956. This was very much an update of the two earlier machines, although it had several worthwhile innovations and a more sporting performance. The engine dimensions were unchanged, but the porting was improved and a larger carb fitted. To make better use of the increased power, a new four-speed gearbox was introduced and its sporting pretensions were heightened by a special performance kit which included handlebars, a tank cushion for 'flat out' riding, a close ratio gear cluster, and improved hydraulic units for the rear suspension.

But 1956 is best remembered for Montesa's third visit to the Isle of Man, when a full works team mounted an attempt for honours. Four riders, Grace, Cama, Gonzales and Sirera, were entered. The TT bikes appeared surprisingly standard, retaining the same bore and stroke measurements, and with twin exhaust pipes using what appeared to be standard silencers. The result was bikes which were uncannily quiet, earning themselves the following comment in *Motor Cycling*: 'Whispering Spanish two-stroke Montesas'. But under the surface things were far from standard. A hint of this came with the giant 30 mm Italian Dell'Orto racing carb. But the

Above
1956 Isle of Man TT. Marcello Cama at speed on the Clypse Course. He finished second behind Carlo Ubbiali (MV). Team mates Gonzales and Sirera were 3rd and 4th

Above right
Montesa privateer Leif Smedn of Sweden (31) and England's Alan Shepherd (MZ) take a spectacular tumble during the 1961 Swedish GP at Kristianstad

Right
Margo Pearson with her Montesa Sportsman production racer at Aberdare Park, 26 August 1961. Did she start the stickers idea?

real giveaway was the gearbox, a special six-speed affair, bolted up and mounted on special alloy plates at the rear of the engine.

Of the four machines Marcello Cama's was the quickest – producing around 18 bhp at the rear wheel and providing a maximum speed in the Island of a shade over 100 mph. Ranged against them in a race staged over the shorter Clypse Circuit were several formidable teams including MV Agusta, FB

Mondial and CZ. But one by one, the supposedly superior four-strokes fell by the wayside, leaving Cama to come home second, followed by his teammates Gonzales and Sirera, in a race won by Carlo Ubbiali and MV. Grace retired with engine troubles.

Throughout the remainder of 1956 and 1957 Montesa continued to gain some highly creditable performances on the race track before quitting the GP scene, ostensibly to concentrate once again on road bike development. In fact, their retirement had been caused by a downturn in the Spanish economy which was placing a heavy financial burden on the company. This retirement from GP racing was also to herald the start of a major disagreement between the partners which ultimately led to a split between them in May 1958. Simply put, Bulto believed it was foolhardy to cut the racing budget, Permanyer quite the reverse . . . so Bulto left to form his own company and so Bultaco was born!

That year also saw Montesa adopt swinging arm rear suspension. By then the Brio 110 – the latest version of the 125 single – had become a truly modern machine with a sleek dual saddle, large drum brakes, a superb finish and a powerful 11.5 bhp engine. But even so Montesa were struggling financially after Permanyer had been forced to purchase Bulto's shareholding.

By the beginning of the 1960's the company was in dire straights; not only had the rival Bultaco concern done well in racing, it had also taken a considerable share of the market, the very sales upon which Montesa depended.

By 1962 it was obvious that Montesa had to fight back or die. And so was born the Impala – named after a publicity stunt which saw three prototypes of the new bike ridden from one end of Africa to the other. The Impala initially had a capacity of 174 cc (60.9 x 60 mm). This proved such a success it not only saved the company but generated additional funds for the development of a sports/racing version and also a new motocross model. The latter was the first Montesa built for purely off-road use and was to chart the future progress of the company. Soon the engine capacity was increased to 247 cc (72.55 x 60 mm).

The Impala's success was so great that a new factory was built later in 1963, for by then production facilities had once again been outstripped. Not only was there a new factory, but also new modern machinery and equipment, making Montesa the most up-to-date engineering plant in Spain.

A 124 cc Montesa at the Snetterton Combine national road races, July 1963

*West German rider Manfred Rahm with his Montesa
175 Impala Sport during the Thruxton 500-mile
endurance race, 20 June 1964*

In May 1965 the Irishman Sammy Miller stunned
the whole motorcycling world by winning the Scottish Six Day Trial on a Bultaco – the first victory in
the event for a non-British bike. Obviously there was
still a large amount of rivalry between the old partners and Permanyer was more stunned than most. It
was another two full years before Montesa could respond. Subsequently, not only did Montesa (and Ossa
for that matter) give their Spanish rival a run for
their money in all branches of off-road sport, but
each entered into a long running and hard fought
technical battle. The resulting improvements and
innovations lifted all three companys' bikes to previously undreamt of heights.

The dirt bike competition also virtually signalled
an end to Montesa's involvement in both road racing
and production roadsters. But not before they had
won the 1966 Montjuich Park Barcelona 24 hour
endurance race (for the third time) and had been
involved with the Italian Villa brothers in new 125
and 250 road racers which owed much to Mondial

who had originally built the machines.

However, even if the factory had largely called it a
day on the tarmac, a number of privateers around
the globe continued to fly the Barcelona factory's
flag at club, national and even international level,
and none more so than the British.

The UK press first laid hands on the 250 Impala
Sport in 1967. Bruce Main-Smith of *Motor Cycling*
took one to Brands Hatch just prior to the 500-mile
production race it had been entered for. He described it as mechanically simple but quick, while
condemning the wildly inaccurate 110 mph speedo
reading. Inaccurate maybe, but it wasn't that far out
as Brian Bedford's Impala was clocked at 105 mph
through the Snetterton speed trap in standard production trim in 1971!

At £249 assembled in 1968, the Impala was pricey,
but in kit form to avoid purchase tax, that came
down to a competitive £197. There was no shortage
of shoe-string racers waiting to take delivery of one
of these red and grey Spanish flyers. Imported
jointly by Thompsons Garages and Montala Motors,
the 250 Impala never enjoyed the same sales success
as the Suzuki T20 or the Honda CB72, but it did
make a top-class production racer.

Above
Oriol Regas, 250 Montesa Impala during the 500
miles race at Brands Hatch, 26 June 1966

Above left
Montesa made an official return to GP racing in 1967
with new machines based on the Mondials raced in
Italy by the Villa brothers. Jose Busquets is shown
here on one of the disc valve 125 singles during the
Spanish GP at Montjuich Park, Barcelona that year

Left
The 1967 Montesa twin. Its 247.3 cc disc valve twin
was capable of over 35 bhp and nearly 130 mph and
its frame was excellent

Built in Montesa's new Barcelona factory, the 248 cc (72.55 x 60 mm) two-stroke was in the true Spanish tradition. The large, three port close-finned alloy cylinder sported a well proportioned cast iron liner and ran a short-skirt Dykes-ringed piston. Its I-section conrod, roller small-end and caged roller big-end could go to 9,000 rpm without being any the worse for the experience. When combined with a rigid, full-circle flywheel assembly and gear primary drive, it all added up to one thing – reliability.

The 26 bhp was taken to the gearbox by a bullet-proof steel and bronze all-metal clutch. With gearbox ratios of 15.18, 18, 10.12, 7.77 and 6.34 it needed to be, as an awful lot of clutch slipping was required to pull away with such a high first gear. However, the only regular failures noticed were in the gearbox. Not many, maybe, but more than a few racers lost a ratio or two.

The 30 mm carb was an Amal Monobloc made under licence in Spain. Jets and spares were easy to obtain, but there were problems. The Spanish device wasn't the same as the Birmingham-built item. They may have looked similar, but the jet holder was completely different, which made the slides and needles different and in fact only jets and a few smaller items were interchangeable. The Impala's 6V flywheel magneto lighting didn't live up to the rest of the bike. To quote a 1967 road test: 'The main light was of adequate brilliance for after dark cruising at 55 mph'. Hardly encouraging, but as most Impalas were destined for the track it didn't matter too much.

As expected, the Montesa manufactured frame, forks and brakes were superb. The very distinctive

leading axle, oil damped forks worked and worked well. But it was the Impala's 180 mm (7 ins) front brake that really signalled its sporting intentions. All alloy with a large air scoop, the full-width twin leading shoe stopper came straight off a race track and, with the aid of Ferodo AM4 linings, could handle the Impala without protest.

With alloy rims as standard and liberal use of plastics, the Impala weighed in at a remarkable 88 kg (227 lb) dry. Just to put that figure into perspective, a modern 125 cc Yamaha or Honda single weighs in at more than this.

During the course of any race machine's life it will undergo a fair amount of modification. One such story is told by Chris McGahan whose antics aboard the Cliff Judge Impala Sport brought him many a trophy. To improve the standard bike, Cliff fitted a 230 cc Ossa caged small-end. This didn't help reliability, but it certainly helped his nerves, as any mechanic who's had to push a gudgeon pin through an uncaged needle roller small end held together only by grease will tell you. In 1972 the original points/magneto was replaced with a Motoplat system. The bike was still eligible for production races as the Motoplat system could be supplied with a 6V direct lighting coil, but unlike the lightweight race version the roadster system used a heavier outside flywheel assembly.

The standard 2.50 x 19 ins front and 2.75 x 19 ins rear wheels normally attracted their share of modifications. Most riders changed to 18 inch rims, not looking for any improvement in the excellent handling but in order to fit the only race tyres available – 18 inch Dunlops. By 1971 Chris' Impala had had quite a bit of engine work done, including a five-port liner, Bultaco TSS piston, and a 32 mm Spanish Monobloc all fitted in the never-ending search for speed and reliability.

There was one change that, surprisingly, didn't give results. A fully tapered expansion box was tried and modified but showed little gain over the standard anti-social front pipe and silencer set up.

And it was with the latter standard set-up fitted that Chris and his Impala scored a dozen outright wins and many placings, so the original Montesa system couldn't have been far off the mark.

Left
Englishman Chris McGahan pilots his Tom Mortimer-tuned Montesa Scorpion to 4th place in the 1973 Barcelona 24-hour race. The British flew the Montesa flag proudly

During early 1972 Chris was approached by Tom Mortimer (destined to become boss of tuning emporium Mel Le Moto and previously an AMC race mechanic) with the idea of modifying a Montesa King Scorpion trial bike for production racing. To show how versatile Montesa singles were, Chris went on to win many class awards on the hybrid, and even took the King Scorpion to fourth place in the 1972 Barcelona 24 hours, a truly remarkable achievement on a machine not at all designed for the prupose.

Other British riders with notable Impala achievements to their names include the Bedford brothers, Alan and Brian. Their Impala was purchased new from Bob Jones Motorcycles in Northampton in May 1968 and had to double up as ride-to-work transport and weekend racer. Obviously, this led to complications, but by 1971 Alan had clocked up some pretty impressive results including the 1970 Bantam Club and Racing 50 production championships. Brother Brian continued the winning streak, taking second place in the Bantam Club championship and third in the 250 production class at the British GP in 1973.

Their machine followed the same path as the others, with a five-port barrel, Motoplat ignition and 18 inch wheels. But it wasn't restricted to road racing. Brian entered the production bike class at the Santa Pod dragstrip and captured the British record in 15.22 seconds. And just to show how quick the little Impala really was, Brian came home tenth in a national open 250 race at Mallory Park against TZ Yamahas and the like.

With the increasing popularity of classic racing, the 250 Impala enjoyed a second run of success. Brian Bedford soon proved that there was life in his old Montesa yet. First time out for five years, he headed John Witt-Man's Ducati and Rob Peabody's TSS Bultaco to take first place at the Classic Racing Motorcycle Club's inaugural meeting back in 1981.

As for Montesa themselves, like the majority of the large Spanish bike builders they hit financial trouble in the early 1980s . . . even their dirt bikes couldn't keep them afloat this time. After first being bailed out by the Spanish government, the Japanese Honda company pumped in some £3 million pounds sterling in 1986, gaining a majority shareholding in Montesa at the same time. In effect Honda now calls the shots at the Barcelona factory.

With Bultaco, Ossa, Sanglas and Mototrans all now extinct this leaves Derbi as the only volume motorcycle manufacturer left in Spain, a truly sad state of affairs and a tragic fall from the great days of the 1950s and 1960s.

OSSA

Spanish industrialist Manuel Giro had a passion for motorcycling; he also owned a large and profitable company. *Orpheo Sincronia SA* manufactured film projectors and other cinema equipment, but under Giro's direction the company's initials were destined to take on another meaning.

Like many others, Giro's interest in motorcycling stemmed from his first two wheeler, originally purchased as basic transport. The year was 1924, and the machine was an American-built Cleveland powered by a 270 cc single cylinder two-stroke.

At the time he brought the Cleveland, Giro was a serving officer in the merchant marine, but after getting married he left the sea and founded his cinema equipment business. This prospered and soon became successful enough for Giro to take up the expensive hobby of power boat racing.

However, two wheels were not entirely forgotten, and in the early 1930s, Giro purchased a Norton. This fed his natural enthusiasm for motorcycling to the point where he soon thirsted for a more potent piece of machinery – and so an ex-works Norton CS1 racer was purchased from Percy Hunt, the English rider who was on a visit to Spain for the Spanish

Grand Prix. Unhappily, Manuel Giro's riding skills did not quite match the performance potential of his latest acquisition, with the result that he fell more times than he finished during his early racing attempts.

By the mid-1930's Giro had changed his allegiance to one of BMW's flat twins, but found the German bike underpowered against the Norton. Some might question the wisdom of his next move, which was to fit a 998 cc supercharged six cylinder overhead cam Soriano engine from one of his power boats to the BMW chassis.

Somehow Giro managed to graft the two together, but can you imagine a massive 112 bhp at 6,000 rpm mounted in a rigid frame with girder forks? If nothing else Manuel Giro could claim the most potent racing motorcycle of its era – and probably the most ill-handling too!

His next move was onto three wheels and sidecar racing, where his enthusiasm at last paid dividends with the result that he became Spanish champion.

The 175 Ossa Sport which, ridden by the pairing of Pedro Millet and Luis Yglesis, won their class in the 1965 Barcelona 24-hour endurance classic

But by then, the clouds of the Civil War which split Spain asunder were darkening the horizon, and with the outbreak of the conflict came an end to all pleasure activities, including racing.

Manuel Giro was forced to turn all his efforts towards seeing his business through the hostilities, which ended in the spring of 1939 leaving General Franco firmly in control of the whole country, in a year when the global conflict of the Second World War began. Although Spain was not directly involved, nonetheless these dark days continued to have an influence on the nation.

Despite these outward preoccupations, Giro's continued enthusiasm for motorcycles led to him turning his hand to design. With the excesses of the Soriano-BMW well and truly behind him, he drew up a 125 cc single cylinder two-stroke. Although this never progressed beyond the prototype stage, it may have played an important role in the birth of the Spanish motorcycle industry, for Giro claims that the engine was in fact given to the fledgling Montesa concern, and that it was used as a basis for getting that marque off the ground in 1945 – even powering its first racing machines.

Noting the success of Montesa and this two-stroke engine, Giro set about the design and construction of his own motorcycle, and it was about this time that the Ossa name first made its bow. The initial model was, not surprisingly, a 123.67 cc (54 x 54 mm) single cylinder two-stroke, but unlike the Montesa machines of the period, it featured a central exhaust pipe which left the port between the twin downtubes of the neat double cradle frame. Producing 5 bhp at 4,500 rpm, the little Ossa's engine drove the bike through a three-speed gearbox to a maximum speed of 47 mph.

From this original model came a whole range of machines which were used both for everyday purposes, and in specially prepared versions that contested the rigours of the ISDT during the 1950s.

An improved eighth-litre model appeared in 1954, followed in 1958 by an enlarged version with a 149.01 cc (58 x 56.4 mm) engine. Next, in the same year, came a 175 four-stroke roadster of Italian influence. But it was back to two-strokes in 1959, when a more sporty variant of the well-tried 125 made its debut. This was the 125C, which featured not only a peppier power output aided by a higher 7.1:1 compression ratio, but also a new duplex frame – clearly based on the GT175 four-stroke. The wheels were reduced to 18 inch diameter whilst the 145 mm (5.6 inch) diameter brakes were superbly effective for such a small, lightweight sportster.

It was with this model that Ossa really displayed a pointer to the factory's participation in future road racing events. The 125C did indeed perform well, and many a young Spaniard of the day lusted after the sporty-looking bike with its lightweight sprung steel mudguards, racing-style tank, narrow seat and low handlebars. A year later, Ossa pursued the theme even further with a still faster, more sporting variant, the C2. Both found their way onto the track in some numbers, but only through private entries with no real factory backing.

The early 1960s was a bad time for the Spanish motorcycle industry, and in common with other Spanish bike builders, Ossa found their sales severely curtailed. The reason was the same as in other countries – Joe Public had discovered the cheap and instantly available small car. However Ossa were to benefit more than most companies, with the arrival of Manuel Giro's son, Eduardo. It was through this man perhaps, more than any other, that Ossa were able to grow through this troubled period and for almost two decades thereafter.

Eduardo was an amazing partner for his father and a huge asset to the company. From the first time he saw a motorcycle, Eduardo had always known what he wanted to do and he had grown into a brilliant designer. His engineering skills were first demonstrated at the age of fifteen when he both drew up and constructed a model aircraft engine. This tiny unit would spin to over 18,000 rpm and it laid the foundations for Eduardo's first commercial design – the 158.53 cc (58 x 60 mm) single cylinder two-stroke of 1962, an engine which was to form the backbone of Ossa production for many years to come.

From this stemmed the 175 cc (60.9 x 60 mm) in 1965, the 230 cc (70 x 60 mm) in 1966 and by joining two singles together, the 488.58 cc (72 x 60 mm) Yankee twin in 1972. Finally the 244.29 cc (72 x 60 mm) single appeared in 1975. These engines also proved extremely versatile, being used at various times in commuter bikes, sports roadsters, production racers, motocross, enduro and trials machines amongst other things.

The first use of the new Eduardo Giro designed engine for racing came with the introduction of the 175 Sport in 1965. In standard roadgoing form it was capable of a genuine 90 mph, producing 19 bhp at 7,200 rpm.

Ossa were confident that the 175 Sport would form an ideal basis with which to contest the local Barcelona 24-hour endurance classic. But at the time most observers viewed the pair of modified roadsters

which came to the grid for the 1965 event as also-rans – surely they stood no chance against such established endurance racing marques as Ducati (Mototrans), Bultaco and Montesa?

The result even surprised Ossa themselves when the two newcomers shook the Spanish racing establishment by taking the first two places in their class. The winning pair of riders, Pedro Millet and Luis Yglesias, between them clocked up an astonishing 584 laps in 24 hours, compared to the total of 631 for the overall winner, a 649 cc Dresda Triton.

Spurred on by this success, Ossa sent the victorious Barcelona team to Britain to contest the Thruxton 500 mile race. Their eventual sixth placing (in class) was excellent, since they were competing against full 250s, such as the Cotton Conquest, Honda CB72 and Ducati Mach 1, all of which had outstanding performance.

Realising that it was giving away some 75 cc, Ossa's next move was to increase the capacity of their Sport to 230 cc. To achieve this, the bore and stroke dimensions were changed to 70 x 60 mm, the cylinder barrel casting redesigned with not only the larger bore but eight instead of seven fins, the compression ratio was lowered to 10:1 and a 27 mm Amal carburettor fitted. These changes resulted in the power output climbing to 23 bhp at 7,000 rpm, but the most noticeable improvement was in superior torque figures.

Carlos Giro, who together with Luis Yglesis scored an amazing overall victory in the 1967 Barcelona marathon on their 230 Ossa Sport

In the 1966 Barcelona 24-hours one of the new 230s finished 3rd in its class and 5th overall; whilst a race-kitted example contested the national 250 cc road racing championships with considerable success, including victory in the important *Gran Premio De Espana* on the 8 May at Montjuich Park, Barcelona.

By this time Ossa, like rivals Bultaco and Montesa, had begun to take an active interest in dirt bike sport, which included trials, motocross and enduro. But despite this, Ossa was still to maintain a considerable presence in the road racing arena.

Overall victory in the Barcelona 24-hour race finally came to Ossa in 1967 when a 230 Sport ridden by Carlos Giro and Luis Yglesias belied its capacity to beat the entire field. In doing this the machine covered 662 laps, a record which was to stand for several years.

The 230 Sport went on to score further successes in sports machine racing, including victory in the 250 cc race of the 1968 Isle of Man Production TT, where an example entered by the British importer and former racer Eric Houseley, and ridden by Trevor Burgess, took victory against the cream of the

production racing brigade. But Ossa, through the work of chief designer Eduardo Giro, had its sights set on greater things in the road racing world – no less than a full crack at Grand Prix honours!

Eduardo had first begun design studies for this machine back in the middle of 1966, but it was quickly realised that the main problem he faced was that Ossa simply did not have enough cash to build a multi-cylinder model which could take on the Japanese at their own game – even though Eduardo Giro was sure that he could have designed such an engine. So right from the start he realised that his GP racer would have to be a single, and because of the

Left
Ossa 250 GP bike as it appeared in 1968. Note alloy monocoque frame and linked rear shocks (the latter feature was soon abandoned for the far more conventional British oil-filled Girling units)

Below
A 1969 shot of the Grand Prix Ossa single without its fairing, showing the massive cylinder finning, 42 mm Amal carb and chassis layout to full advantage

Above
Santiago Herrero at speed during the 1969 Isle of Man TT. He came home in 3rd spot

Below
Nearside details of Ossa engine showing cylinder, clutch, ignition and exhaust

factory policy, it would also have to be a two-stroke.

It was obvious to Eduardo that power-to-weight ratio and a small frontal area would be all-important. Like the 1950's Moto Guzzi 350, or Tarquinio Provini's incredible Morini, these principles would have to dominate the design, coupled with exceptional roadholding. Finally, the racer must achieve a high standard of reliability, so that a maximum number of finishes could be achieved by a single rider, as once again finance ruled out a team of several pilots.

A tall order, especially for a firm with a living to earn, but by late 1966 a prototype engine unit had been completed and was already on the testbed. Early the following year it had been installed in a frame and the complete racer was being given its initial track testing – much of the early riding development being carried out by the 1967 Barcelona 24-hour race victor Carlos Giro.

The heart of any motorcycle is its engine, and here Eduardo Giro was forced to move away from Ossa's traditional simple piston port induction, opting instead for the greater precision of a disc valve. All Eduardo's skill in the black art of two-stroke technology was needed to give the Ossa GP the kind of competitive edge it needed if the Spanish single cylinder machine was to have a chance against the might of Japan.

Of course a disc valve alone counted for nothing against machines like the V4 Yamaha. And the more one studies the Ossa GP engine, the more incredible it seems that Giro persevered with the major efforts involved in creating what must have seemed at times an impossible dream.

The 249 cc air-cooled engine had a bore and stroke of 70 x 65 mm. The seven fin barrel and head had such large fins that the top end looked more like a 500 than a 250. Its carburettor was a massive 42 mm Amal, fitted on the right-hand crankcase. Equally large was the expansion chamber exhaust, which exited on the left and was secured to the barrel by four springs – simple but efficient, these twin themes echoed throughout the bike. Ignition was electronic, by Motoplat. Even though the maximum power was, by 1969, some 42 bhp at 11,000 rpm, useful power was generated as far down the rev-band as a reputed 6,500 rpm, making the machine's six-speed gearbox quite sufficient.

The power unit was mounted in an unorthodox and technically very interesting sheet alloy monocoque frame assembly. This was ideal for its purpose, being light yet super strong and endowed the machine with superb roadholding abilities. This monocoque also incorporated the fuel tank, part of

keeping the weight and height down to a minimum. The engine was suspended below the frame in the manner of some of Ossa's earlier road machines, supported at the cylinder head and the rear of the crankcases.

The rest of the cycle parts were unremarkably conventional. The swinging arm was fabricated from elongated steel tube, front and rear suspension were proprietary Telesco components, while the brakes appeared to be those from the roadster 230 Sport model. The total dry weight of the prototype was just 97.5 kg (215 lb), but this was ultimately to rise to 99 kg (219 lb) when 38 mm Ceriani racing front forks, Girling rear shocks and Italian racing brakes were substituted. The stoppers used in this form included a massive 240 mm four leading shoe front brake.

The 250 GP single's first race was at the 1967 Spanish Grand Prix, when in front of a local crowd, Carlos Giro rode it to a splendid debut finish in 6th position. This might have pleased many designers, but not Eduardo Giro. In this, he had some reason, for the Spanish event did not place a premium on outright speed. On his reckoning, only a finish near the front of the field on such a twisting circuit would show that the bike had true race-winning potential.

For 1968, the factory secured the services of the Spanish 250 champion Santiago Herrero. In Herrero, Ossa had not only signed up one of the finest riders ever produced by Spain, but also gained someone with a flair for being able to assess exactly what development work was needed and the skill to transmit that vital information back to the designer.

His first race outing for Ossa was the 1968 West German Grand Prix at the Nürburgring, where even though many changes had been made to the bike it was still not quite quick enough. However, by the time of the Spanish round, it was good enough for Herrero to lead the race until forced to retire with engine problems – and this against the Yamaha V4s of Phil Read and Bill Ivy. Even so, second string rider Carlos Giro upheld the marque's honour with a very creditable 4th place.

At the Isle of Man TT, Herrero's first ever race over the difficult 37¾-mile mountain circuit, his Ossa came in 7th. But this was followed by ever-improving results: a 6th at the Dutch TT, a 5th at the ultra-fast Belgian TT, and a brilliant 3rd in the Italian GP at Monza. Although not able to compete in

Overleaf
Herrero on his way to victory in the 1969 250 cc Belgian GP. His winning average speed for the eight lap 70 mile race was 117.96 mph

After the 250 cc race of the 1969 Belgian GP. Left to right: *Rod Gould (2nd), Santiago Herrero (winner) and Kel Carruthers (3rd)*

all the qualifying rounds that year, the Spanish rider and the Spanish machine still finished 7th in the 250 cc world championships.

Herrero's fiery riding and the speed and reliability of the air-cooled Ossa single meant that they won three of the 1969 Grand Prix rounds (Spain, France and Belgium), also gaining a 3rd place in the IoM TT at an average of 92.82 mph. These were amazing results for such a small factory with slim resources and they startled the racing world. Ossa completed the final season of the 1960's in third place in the championship, showing just what could be achieved by two determined men – a gifted engineer and a brilliant rider.

As the new decade opened, it seemed as if Herrero and the Ossa single could go on to make a much greater mark on the racing history books. By 1970 the power output had been pushed even higher, to an amazing 45 bhp. This figure was achieved when the engine was still in its air-cooled form, although the previous year during practice for the Dutch TT at

Assen, it had appeared in an experimental form with a water-cooled head and barrel. In the end, Herrero had opted for the original air-cooled version for the race and had continued to use it in subsequent events.

So it was as the Spanish challenger came to the grid for the 1970 Isle of Man TT. Many eyes were on the sleek monocoque framed single and its hard rider, who were tipped to spring a surprise on the racing establishment. All seemed set for an even higher placing than the year before, when the Ossa sped through the electronic speed trap at the Highlander section at 137.9 mph (against 133.3 mph in 1969). This speed was third fastest in the class – only surpassed by Paul Smart's Yamaha and the MZ of Gunter Bartusch.

But tragedy struck on the first lap, as Santiago Herrero reached the fast left hander at the base of the downhill 13th milestone section. Caught out by molten tar on the road surface, he lost control of the Ossa, crashed heavily and was fatally injured. The accident struck at the heart of the Ossa factory, and deeply affected Eduardo Giro in particular. As a result, the firm withdrew from the world championship, and never again competed officially.

7
Sweden

Sweden is somewhat unusual in the annals of motorcycle racing; for one thing tarmac racing is usually held in warmer climes, which an outdoor sport is better suited to. But of course there is an exception to every rule and Sweden has long been engaged in a love affair with all forms of motorcycle (and motor) sport. For example, consider just how many world champions on both two and four wheels have come from that country.

Although there were others, it was Husqvarna and the MCB group of companies (including Monark, Cresent and NL who dominated the Swedish motorcycle industry; both being able to trace their history right back to the turn of the century. And although the Scandinavian country is world famous for its many world-beating off road bikes, it also built some surprisingly good tarmac racers too, both before and after the Second World War.

For many years the national Grand Prix was staged over the now defunct Hedemora circuit, but later it was staged over first Kristianstad and, later still, Anderstorp.

Husqvarna

The history of the Husqvarna factory and the development of their motorcycles is a long and interesting story. It started way back in 1699 when Erik Dahlberg, a leading industrialist and governor of the region in which the town of Huskvarna (note the 'k' in place of the 'q') was situated, decided to supply much-needed weapons to the Swedish army. In those days Sweden was constantly engaged in conflicts with her Scandinavian neighbours, and with business brisk the factory grew at a rapid pace.

Unfortunately the Swedish King, Carl XII, decided to wage war on Russia and though output reached new heights while the battle was on, a massive depression hit the Husqvarna company when the Russians emerged victorious.

For many years after that the works just about managed to keep its head above water, and in 1867 it was reorganised and given the name under which it traded until the motorcycle division was sold to the Italian Cagiva company in the mid-1980s, *Husqvarna Vapenfabriks AB*.

Then came more wars and business was again good; its location at the centre of Sweden's southern tip, a good position to ship arms to Denmark and Germany, was also a great help.

After the Franco-Prussian war of the early 1870s the Husqvarna management began to seek out more peaceful products. As they were used to high-precision engineering, they started to manufacture sewing machines – and this venture was a success, leading to the famous line of Husqvarna/Viking sewing machines.

Steadily the business continued to expand and when the motor age hit the world Husqvarna were quick to seize their opportunity; in 1903 they began to produce motorcycles using a Swiss designed Moto-Reve engine.

The next major step came in 1918 when Husqvarna designed and built their own complete machines for the very first time. A big contract for the Swedish Army followed and the motorcycle side became an important money-spinner. It was also around this time that the 'Husky' marque made its first moves into motorcycle sport. This had come two years earlier when L E Ringborg had won the famous *Novemberkasan* cross country race on one of the company's 550 cc v-twin models.

Quickly realising that competition wins were the finest form of publicity, Husqvarna stepped up their interest and developed special machines for the long distance cross country events then popular throughout Scandinavia. These in turn led to Husqvarna bikes appearing in the International Six Days Trial.

In the early thirties Husqvarna sporting interests turned to road racing, which had blossomed into a major sport with vast crowds turning out to watch the Grand Prix races being staged in almost every country throughout Europe. The young engineer Folke Mannersted had returned to Sweden to join the factory from the Belgian FN concern in 1928 and one of his first tasks was the construction of a new racer powered by a British JAP single cylinder overhead valve engine with which Husqvarna could join the Grand Prix circus. The machine had a displacement of 493.6 cc (85 x 87 mm). Maximum power was 31 bhp at 6,000 rpm and it could touch almost 100 mph. Unfortunately this machine, together with a 250 cc version, were simply not powerful enough for the Swedes to challenge the likes of Norton, Rudge or Sunbeam.

After indifferent results, Mannersted set out to build an all-new engine. This time it had two cylinders arranged in a vee configuration which ran longitudinally. This first prototype appeared at the 1930 Swedish Grand Prix at Saxtorp, but although Yagve Eriksson came home third, the new bike was neither fast enough nor reliable enough to challenge the all-powerful Norton team led by Jimmy Simpson for the major honours.

Two years on from its debut the v-twin suddenly emerged as a serious challenger for the European championship when Ragnar Sunnqvist won the local GP, defeating in the process the best that the other works teams could muster.

The 497.7 cc (65 x 75 mm) ohv 50 degree angle v-twin pumped out 44 bhp at 6,800 rpm and was good for around 120 mph. With this sort of performance it is easier to understand why there followed three great years when the Swedish marque with riders such as Ragnar Sunnqvist, Gunnar Kalen, Yagve Eriksson and that great Irish rider, Stanley Woods, mounted an effective challenge to the British monopoly of the 500 cc class. But it was not until 1932 that the bike proved to be a race winner, with Kalen emerging as Husqvarna's leading rider with countless wins and lap records throughout 1933 on the Swedish 500 v-twin.

In 1934 the team suffered some cruel blows of fate, even though their machines were much improved. The lorry carrying its load of bikes to the TT was dropped from its crane onto the Gothenburg quayside, thus damaging its cargo. But this was nothing compared to the loss of two of their riders. Gunnar Kalen was killed at the German GP, and the Belgian rider Van der Pluym died at the Belgian GP that year. These tragic events set the scene for the great Norton star, Irishman Stanley Woods, to join the promising Swedish team. The tragedies did not stop Husqvarna making a real impact, with Ernie Nott

winning the Junior TT and Woods holding second in the Senior before running out of fuel on the last lap. The weather had been terrible, but he still set the fastest lap at 80.49 mph. Woods even came off and got back on again at Ramsey Hairpin. If the fuel had not run out the team would have had the intense pleasure of splitting the one-two victory of the works Nortons of Jimmy Guthrie and Jimmy Simpson. This was all the more amazing when all that had remained after the quayside incident was a few bent frames and forks. The whole lot had been rushed back to the factory, where Mannersted worked his magic on them. The machines for that year were 350 and 500 cc; on the larger mount the compression ratio was up from 7.3:1 to 9.5:1 and better valves and a stiffened crankcase resulted in 46 bhp.

The engine was fairly conventional in that the crankcase was vertically separated and with push-rod tubes on the right-hand side and the rockers were exposed. There were two carburettors squeezed into the vee of the cylinders, angled to give a down-draught effect. There were exceptionally long (extending way behind the rear wheel) exhausts and ignition was by Bosch magneto mounted on the front of the engine. Transmission was via a Sturmey-Archer four-speed gearbox, selection being obtained by a rocking pedal on the right-hand side. The rigid frame remained, as did the girder forks. The weight was kept below 127 kg (280 lbs), remarkable at the time due to the extensive use of light alloy.

With their hero Kalen dead, a lot of the fizz went out of the Husqvarna racing effort, but they continued into 1935; and while Stanley Woods switched to a Guzzi v-twin to win the Senior TT, the Irishman reverted to a Husky for the Swedish Grand Prix to score yet another classic victory (the company's fourth consecutive win in the event).

At the end of 1935 Husqvarna officially quit the GP scene however, the machines were lent out and raced under the 'Scuderia Husqvarna' banner by Ragnar Sunnqvist and other Swedish riders. But the great days were over, for with the latest Nortons and the new supercharged BMWs going ever faster there was no chance of success for a design which wasn't undergoing constant development.

Soon after they stopped racing Husqvarna discontinued building 350 and 500 cc roadsters and instead concentrated their efforts on smaller, lighter bikes. Post-war this process continued with new two-strokes of 98, 118 and 174 cc. In addition, the factory returned to off-road sport, first the ISDT and later motocross.

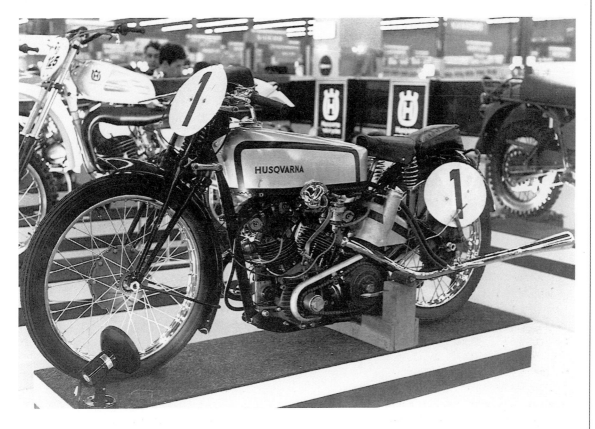

The legendary Husqvarna 500 v-twin which was raced with such success by men such as Gunnar Kalen and Stanley Woods in the early and mid-1930's

It was in the early 1950s when motocross first came to Sweden, spreading across the continent of Europe from Belgium where the sport had taken a firm commercial footing in 1946 and 1947. At first private owners modified the standard 175 Husqvarna roadster to race, but with the introduction of the 250 cc European motocross championship (called the *Coupe d'Europe*) Husqvarna began to take a more active interest.

Their first works rider in the contest was Rolf Tibblin, who appeared in several rounds during 1958. The following season Rolf and his Husky really came into their own, winning the title after a great tussle with the Greeves rider Brian Stonebridge. From then on Husqvarna were to become one of the mainstays of motocross and enduro racing, with a string of international victories and championships. Although outside the scope of this book, it would be true to say that Husqvarna dominated the off-road racing scene for much of the 1960s and in the process played a vital role in the development of both sports on a world-wide basis.

Amongst all this success on the dirt, Husqvarna engineers still managed to find the time to retain a level of interest in road racing. The first positive hint of this came in the summer of 1964 when a two-fifty powered by a single cylinder two-stroke appeared.

Built from parts of a motocross machine, there were plans that if it proved successful, it would become the prototype of a pukka racing model. The 244 cc (69.5 x 64.5 mm) piston port engine used an alloy cylinder head and barrel, the latter with a cast-iron liner. Carburation was taken care of by an Amal GP instrument and ignition was by Bosch coil and battery. Initial power output was 25 bhp – later upped to around the 30 bhp mark. Surprisingly the frame intended for off-road work, was found to be just as suitable for road racing. The tank of this first post-war tarmac racer was appropriately patterned on the famous pre-war Husqvarna racing twins; the prototype machine was sponsored by the magazine *MC-Nytt*.

Outside Scandinavia nothing much was heard of this project until the 1966 Spanish GP at Montjuich Park, Barcelona. It was there that the factory wheeled out a couple of machines which, although slow by comparison with the latest Japanese machinery, nonetheless proved ideal for the twisting Barcelona circuit. Husqvarna's number one rider was a

Left
Motocross based 250 single ridden by Kent Andersson
to 7th place in the 1966 Spanish Grand Prix

Above
Andersson's machine with the fairing removed
displaying its simple construction. Engine produced
around 30 bhp

certain Kent Andersson (later a world champion with Yamaha in 1973 and 1974) who finished a fine seventh; the other rider, Anders Bengtsson, finished tenth.

It should be stated that the bikes were 'semi-works' – being funded partly by the factory and partly by various private enthusiasts.

The machines which had the handicap of having the standard issue wide ratio four-speed gearbox from the motocrosser had earlier in the year finished first and third at the Skarpnack Swedish champion-ship races near Stockholm, sandwiching the ex-champion Bo Brolin and his five-speed Aermacchi. A 500 cc vertical twin Husqvarna engine mounted in a Featherbed frame also made its debut at Skarpnack, ridden by Sigurd Forsell.

As if all this activity was not enough, Forsell also built and raced a 350 cc single cylinder model. As on the 250s, the engine was constructed from motocross components. But unlike the other machines the 350 was fitted in an old MV Agusta frame.

Forsell was soon gaining results too, finishing fifth at Knutstrop in May that year, at a round of the Swedish championship. In the same month, riding his semi-works Husky, Kent Andersson won the 250 class at Mouscron in Belgium on Sunday 22 May. His team mate Anders Bengtsson finished second.

Even better was to come. In August 1966 three 250 Husqvarnas were entered for the Finnish GP and one, ridden by Kent Andersson, finished sixth. They had been steadily improved since earlier in the sea-

Far left
The Husqvarna 500 twin raced by Sigurd Forsell in the 1966 Swedish National Championships; cycle parts were Manx Norton

Below far left
Forsell's five-hundred Husky motor. Pushing out over 50 bhp it had a maximum speed comparable with a standard Matchless G50 or Manx Norton, but superior acceleration

Left
Another Husqvarna raced by Sigurd Forsell was this 348 cc single, housed in an old MV Agusta frame, summer 1966

Below
The English rider Percy Tait in action with one of the semi-works 250 Husqvarnas at Mallory Park, 5 March 1967. Tait was a heat winner on the machine that day

son and were now giving an additional 2 bhp, making a total of 32 horses. Andersson also rode the twin engined model originally raced by Sigurd Forsell; reputed to be pushing out well over 50 bhp, its acceleration was certainly impressive but it failed to last the race.

A privately entered 250, ridden rather spectacularly by the Finn Teuvo Länsivuori (later to campaign Yamaha and Suzuki machines with considerable success in the 1970's), attracted much attention. No wonder his angles of lean defied gravity – he was formerly an ice racer of some note and this was only his second road race!

In 1967 Brian Leask, the British Husqvarna importer, added his weight to the road racing effort. Initially the veteran Percy Tait was provided with one of the semi-works 250s which he raced at Mallory Park and Brands Hatch at the beginning of the season. Later Leask engaged leading club rider Robin Bowler to race 250 and 350 Leask-built Husqvarna racers. These were campaigned at various British circuits that year, plus the Manx Grand Prix with a fair level of success.

On the international stage Bo Granath rode a 348 cc single all over Europe, including a couple of visits to Britain. The same rider later built a 500 Husqvarna special, powered by a pair of 250 cc motocross engines coupled side by side. Once again this was a semi-works effort with the engineering carried out by Helmin Reuben of Husqvarna. The engine in 1968 form gave 55 bhp at 7,500 rpm and appeared to offer considerable potential.

Into 1969 and Granath had two new bikes. One was a developed version of the 500. The other was a completely new 350 cc job. Although the smaller engine didn't prove a success the larger unit was both rapid and reasonably reliable. At its heart was a

Right
Bowler with the 350 Leask-Husqvarna at Silverstone in the summer of 1967

Below right
Bo Granath on the works 350 Husqvarna at Oulton Park, September 1967

Below
British Husqvarna importer Brian Leask built 244 and 346 cc racers for Robin Bowler. Here's the smaller model at Brands Hatch in late February 1967

piston ported 490 cc (69.5 x 64.5 mm) air-cooled twin which by the end of 1969 was giving 60 bhp at 7,800 rpm. Carburettors were twin 35 mm BVF instruments with Amal float bowls. Primary drive was by gears to a five-plate clutch running in oil. Split vertically, and transversely, the forward section at the crankcase was detachable to allow the crankshaft to be removed without disturbing the four-speed gearbox.

With a dry weight of only 120 kg (246 lb), the effort needed to flick the bike through corners was negligible; this also provided an excellent power-to-weight ratio and is the reason why 60 bhp could provide a maximum speed of some 135 mph.

Ultimately a leap in the sales of its off-road machinery in north America halted further development of this interesting machine, but not before serious consideration was given to building an enduro version for use in the United States. But Husqvarna never took this option and so the 500 twin project was quietly shelved and with it went all hopes of a return to past glories in road racing by the famous old Swedish marque.

MCB

By the early 1970's MCB – Monark Crescent AB-could claim to be the largest manufacturer of motorcycles in Sweden, if not the most famous.

MCB actually embraced many famous Swedish marques, even though the company did not actually begin motorcycle manufacture with Monark emblazoned on the tank until 1925, but in reality she had been in the bike business for many years, by way of older marques absorbed into the MCB group along the way and with the import of various foreign products.

The first group company to manufacture motorcycles was Nordstjernan in 1902. And prior to the outbreak of the First World War in 1914 marques such as FN, Puch, NSU, Harley Davidson and Moto Reve were being imported.

The year 1920 saw a new concern 'Esse' making 175 cc class machines, which in 1925 became the first Monarks. A year later Nymans, yet another MCB outfit, commenced production at Uppsala, and in the years which followed they brought out some very attractive models, which were not only pretty, but fast, as witness the machine ridden by Erik Bohlen to victory in the very first Swedish GP in 1930.

In 1926 Monark had begun to use the popular British Blackburne 250 sidevalve engine. In 1928 the company expanded the range of four-strokes to include 350, 500 and 600 cc models; while in 1932

Billy Andersson with the factory 500 Monark-Crescent; Belgian GP, 6 July 1969

The three-cylinder water-cooled two-stroke Crescent racing engine. Its origins came from marine use

Top
Brands Hatch 17 February 1968, Peter Humber's 500
Crescent powered special

Above
Another British built Crescent-powered special; note
reversed cylinders giving front mounted carbs

Above
The Rudi Kurth/Dane Rowe Monark-Crescent Cat sidecar outfit, circa 1972

Below
Engine layout in Kurth machine, with near horizontal cylinders

Nymans (now shortened to NV) introduced their *Volkswagen* bike – designed to be a machine for everyone. More than 40,000 of these were sold before the outbreak of the Second World War in 1939. Before this, in 1936, Monark launched what would later be termed a moped for the mass market.

The coming of the war saw Monark manufacturing 98 and 118 cc models, and NV a full size 125. But development of these soon stopped and production switched to military bikes. The fact that Sweden was not actually involved in the hostilities seems to have had little effect upon this move. The result was that Monark built a brand new army motorcycle entirely from Swedish components. This was achieved in 1942 when a 500 cc ohv single made its bow.

Meanwhile, NV were being even more adventurous in their design brief, the result appearing one year later in the shape of a new 1,000 cc v-twin and sidecar. The specification included no less than eight gears, including a reverse and shaft drive final drive.

Finally, peacetime came and with it a return to the civilian lightweight market. Both Monark and NV mainly used imported engines during this period, including units from the likes of Ilo, DKW and Sachs.

Then, in 1959, Monark rolled out a new 500 cc class motocrosser with Sten Lundin aboard. The result was the 500 cc European championship, but shortly after this both Monark and NV disappeared from the motorcycle scene as the bottom fell out of the Swedish motorcycle market for roadgoing machines. Both MCB group companies were forced to diversify into other commercial activities to remain solvent. Happily the late 1960s saw a resurgence of interest in motorcycles, the result being that Monark, if not NV, returned to the scene in 1967.

As far as the road racing story goes there are two important names: Monark and Crescent – hence the Monark-Crescent name at the beginning of this section. For their 1967 return there were two factories involved: one for motorcycles, mopeds and bicycles, the other for all kinds of boats. Both were situated at Varberg on the beautiful west coast of Sweden.

Much of the impetus for Monark-Crescent came from Ove Lundell, a former member of the national

Dane Rowe and Rudi Kurth after winning the Hutchinson 100, Brands Hatch 6 August 1972 – the first time that the Kent circuit was used in the 'wrong direction'

motocross squad. Not only was Lundell a rider of rare talent, but he was also a brilliant technician. Many of the machines which followed over the next few years were due to the efforts of this man who served the company in the roles of designer, tester and development engineer.

Although Monark-Crescent was mainly involved in the production of lightweight roadsters, mopeds and off-road motorcycles, they still managed to find time to compete in road racing from 1967 until the mid-1970s in such diverse classes as 50, 125 and 500 cc and sidecar. But it was the 50 cc and sidecar cate-

Left
Superbly crafted 49 cc Monark Grand Prix racer, 1973

Below left
Tiny Monark 49 cc disc valve two-stroke single. Note British Gardner flat slide carb and rearward facing exhaust

Below
Nearside view of Monark engine; electronic ignition was by the German Krober company

gories with which they enjoyed most success.

Unlike their production machines which by the late sixties used either German Sachs or Italian Franco Morini engines, the 50 cc and sidecar racers employed engines of Swedish design and construction – although the tiddler was loosely based on an original Sachs layout.

The first road racer appeared in 1967, a 500 cc solo powered by a three cylinder Crescent two-stroke engine originally intended for marine use. It was in fact one of the first attempts to use a boat engine in a racing motorcycle an idea taken up most notably the Berlin based König company (see *Classic German Racing Motorcycles* Osprey Publishing).

Billy Andersson was the first rider to race-test the new 498 cc (60 x 58.8 mm) Monark-Crescent. His 1967 programme included some of the classics, such as the Belgian GP in July.

Besides the factory-backed effort the British Crescent marine importer, Ryan Marine of Southend, Essex was involved in both solo and sidecar racing machines powered by the three cylinder Swedish two-stroke. Ryan's first success came when three-wheel racer Eric Parkinson finished 11th in the 1967 Isle of Man Sidecar TT.

In standard racing specification form the Crescent outboard engine had a power output of 64 bhp at 7,500 rpm, running on a compression ratio of 14:1. Pistons were slightly domed and there were three transfer ports per cylinder. The water pump was belt-driven from the crankshaft, outboard of the Stefa triple contact breaker assembly.

Ryan also supplied an engine which was built as a lightweight solo special during the 1967/68 closed season by Bill Day, John Carpenter and Peter Humber. This was followed by an improved version named the Mistral which appeared a year later; a planned 350 version did not materialise.

After this nothing much was heard of any Monark-Crescent racing until the summer of 1971, when a revised version of the factory-built solo impressed spectators and competitors alike at the 1971 Swedish Grand Prix it was ridden into seventh place by the relatively inexperienced Morgan Radberg. By then the engine was reported to be producing around 67 bhp.

The same year saw the debut of the Cat-Crescent sidecar outfit raced by the Swiss driver Rudi Kurth and his English female passenger Dane Rowe. Their best placing in the classics that year was a fourth at Imata, Finland.

By 1974, Kurth had switched his efforts to engineer rather than competitor and future world champion Rolf Biland was provided with the 'Cat'. His best placing was a superb second to Klaus Enders in the Italian GP at Imola.

Rudi Kurth also built a solo racer with a semi-kneeler riding position in late 1973. This was tested by several top riders including Bruno Kneubuhler, Werner Pfirter and Britain's Mick Grant. After riding the Kurth Monark at Mallory Park, Grant commented that: 'The suspension was not set up right – and in any case it is so low it requires an entirely different technique from a normal bike: I don't think I could do it justice and race my Yamaha so I doubt if I'll ride it again – but it is very fast, I was passing Yamahas down the straight'.

Kurth's specification included a claimed 75 bhp, five-speed Quaife gearbox, a total weight with fairing of only 91 kg (200 lb), Elgi magnesium wheels, twin disc front and single disc rear and gas-hydraulic rear shocks.

But with the advent of faster multi-cylinder two-strokes from Japan, the Monark-Crescent 500 cc three cylinder in both two and three wheel form faded from the scene. Some of this was also due to the fact that Monark as a motorcycle manufacturer ceased production at the end of 1974.

Before this however there had been one final racing project. This was a 50 cc racer which made its debut in 1971 and responded by taking the 50 cc Swedish road racing championship that year. This time it was a pukka factory-backed effort and was seen by many observers as a glimmer of hope in a class which was suffering from a distinct lack of factory machinery to challenge the all-conquering Van Veen Kreidlers and Spanish Derbis.

In their first Grand Prix season the new Swedish tiddlers proved that although beautifully prepared and looking superb, they were no match for the leading bikes in a straight line. Even so Kurt-Ivan Carlsson managed a fourth place in the Yugoslav Grand Prix. This put him 15th in the championship table, a place he shared with his team-mate Lars Persson.

The following year, 1973, the Monarks gained several top six finishes, with a 4th and 5th at the Dutch round (Bruins and Persson) as the highlight. Factory cut-backs meant that there were no bikes available for 1974 and so the Monark challenge came to an end. Persson was also national champion that year.

Even though the controlling MCB group continued to build outboard motors and pedal cycles, both for home market consumption and export, there were to be no more motorcycles. Yet another segment of European motorcycle racing had passed into history.

Monark's leading rider, Lars Persson racing the 50 in Sweden during 1973

8
Yugoslavia

For 1961 the FIM decided to stage the *Coupe d'Europe* (European championship series) in the 50 cc class; this to serve as a forerunner for a full world championship series which was planned for the following season.

A total of eight race organisers ran rounds for the *Coupe d'Europe* during 1961 – three in Belgium, two in Germany and one each for Holland, Spain and Yugoslavia. This final country hardly seemed a likely candidate, at least until the two leading contenders emerged as the West German Kreidler factory and the Yugoslav Tomos company. And although Kreidler and their star rider Hans-Georg Anscheidt eventually emerged as champions, the little known Tomos team put up a tremendous fight, which included winning at the ultra-fast Hockenheim circuit on the Germans' home territory.

Tomos

Based in the small fishing town of Koper a few kilometres south of Trieste on the Adriatic coast, the state-owned Tomos concern had built its business on the manufacture, under licence agreements, of Puch two-wheelers from Austria and automobiles from Citroën of France.

The machine ridden by works rider Miros Zelnik into first place at Hockenheim in 1961 was very much a modified Puch-type moped with semi-horizontal cylinder. A single cylinder two-stroke with conventional piston port induction, the engine unit was modified by fitting a five-speed close ratio gear cluster, special cylinder head and an equally special cylinder barrel in aluminium, finned horizontally, *a la* Moto Guzzi. Carburation was taken care of by a pukka racing Italian Dell'Orto SS instrument with remote float chamber; whilst the exhaust system was very long, with a slender elegant expansion chamber. Maximum speed was in the region of 75–80 mph depending upon gearing. Tomos claimed 8 bhp at 11,000 rpm which seems about right. These results indicate that the Tomos development team were as good as the best at that time.

For 1962, and a full crack at world championship honours, the Tomos engineers headed by Ing. Imperl came up with an all-new effort which owed nothing to the Puch heritage. Coded D7-62 (seven-speed – 1962), the heart of the newcomer was an entirely original engine unit; this sported a vertical cylinder and seven gears, with the clutch running at engine speed. But the features of most interest were hidden inside the engine itself, which was constructed on the nearside of the gearbox. Lubrication was by pump at the bottom end, the dual contact breaker assembly running at half engine speed, whilst the crankshaft flywheel assembly was of double diameter to obtain greater volumetric efficiency via less crankcase volume. But most unusual of all was the aluminium piston without any piston rings or even hardened stainless rubbing coils, which ran in a 38 mm plated alloy cylinder bore.

Sporting the largest carburettor (23 mm) in the class and capable of peaking at 12,000 rpm, the D7-62 was ready for its debut at none other than the very first round of the 1962 50 cc World Championship series at Montjuich Park, Barcelona.

On a lovely sunny morning the Spanish GP, organised by the *Real Moto Club de Cataluna* and held within a mile of the centre of Barcelona, got under way just after 9 o'clock in the morning on Sunday 6 May with the 12 lap, 28.29 mile 50 cc event. The top marques from 1961 – Kreidler and Tomos – were both expected to show up well against the might of the works entries from Honda, Suzuki and the local Derbi concern. But, unfortunately for the Yugoslavian team, the two D7-62s entered both struck gearbox problems; although the Italian Gilberto Parlotti still managed to bring his machine home in 9th spot.

On to the French GP at Clermont Ferrand a week later and the weather couldn't have been more

Three Tomos 50's of the type used by the factory in the 1961 Coupe d'Europe

For 1962, and a full crack at world championship honours, the Tomos engineers, headed by Ing Imperl came up with the all-new D7-62 (seven-speed 1962).

different – bitterly cold and wet. About the only duplication was the Tomos result – another 9th; this time the rider being Roberto Picaga. Team-mate Parlotti came home 17th. Both riders again suffered gearbox gremlins which effectively ruined their chances.

Next round on the championship trail was the Isle of Man TT, but although Tomos originally planned to enter two machines they never put in an appearance and no D7-62 ever took part in an international race again. Instead, Tomos decided to scrap the bikes and return to their original Puch-based design, and it was to be another two years before the Yugoslav team re-entered the arena.

News of the latest developments came when the Australian privateer, Ron Robinson, visited the Tomos factory where he was able to test an experimental racer. This particular machine was a rotary valve two-stroke with duplex frame and five speeds. Robinson also saw a number of Puch-based production racers awaiting despatch to customers not just in Yugoslavia but also in Holland. In the latter country Ferdinand Swaep was to gain many victories during the 1960's on Tomos machinery and became national champion on more than one occasion. This also led ultimately to the Dutch becoming Tomos' main export market, a situation that exists to this day.

At the end of 1964 came news that Tomos racing machines would be imported into Britain by Bolton, Lancashire dealer, John Pomfret. Father of schoolboy road racer Mike Pomfret who at 16 years of age was the proud owner of a dohc Honda CR110, Pomfret Snr had plans to import the 50 cc Tomos production racer into Britain during 1965 at a price well under £200. The plan came following a 1,450 mile overland journey to the Tomos factory in Yugoslavia by John Pomfret in his J D Pomfret & Son dealership's van.

Although the works bike seen by Robinson was disc valve induction, the production racer employed simple piston porting. The capacity of 47.633 cc used 38 mm bore and 42 mm stroke dimensions. The alloy cylinder had a chromed bore and there was a comprehensive (and well made) one-piece expansion chamber exhaust system.

Running on an 11:1 compression ratio maximum power output was 8 bhp at 8,500 rpm. No rev counter was fitted, but Tomos claimed the engine to be virtually unburstable and able to exceed 10,000 rpm with safety. There was a cut-out button on the handlebars enabling the rider to carry out clutchless gear changes.

The balance of the machine was spartan to say the

*One of the Tomos D7-62 racers seen at the Spanish
Grand Prix, 29 April 1962*

*British dealer John Pomfret visited the Yugoslav
factory in the autumn of 1964. Left to right: an
interpreter, Mr Vrecko (export), Mr Stuk (sales),*

*Mr Pomfret, Ing Imperl (racing designer), Ing Miheve
(production designer) and Mr Milcinovic (head of
export department)*

Top
In 1969, Tomos fielded a three-man squad for the 50 cc world series comprising: Gilberto Parlotti, Janko Stefe and Adrijan Bernetic

Above
The 1969 works 50 cc Tomos showing its beam frame, Puch type engine, radiator and the double sided drum front brake

least, with a pressed steel frame, spindly suspension and a mixture of moped-type components making up the balance. Steel rimmed wheels featured neat full-width alloy brakes and 2.00 x 19 ins Continental tyres (these needed replacement before any serious competition could take place). Dry weight, complete with dolphin fairing was only 44.5 kg (98 lb). Hardly awe-inspiring specifications, but out on the circuit the tiny Tomos proved capable of 83 mph on optimum gearing and a match for any production 50 of the era, save the much costlier and exotic Honda CR110.

Tomos continued development of both its works and production 50s during much of the remainder of the 1960s, and towards the end of the decade they were rewarded with placings, even in the world championship series.

In the first round of the 1968 series, at the Nürburgring, West Germany, the Yugoslav rider J Florjan-Steve came home 6th. Inspired by this result, Tomos fielded a three-man squad for the 1969 series comprising: Gilberto Parlotti, Janko Stefe and Adrijan Bernetic. Parlotti started off in fine style with a 4th place in Spain, a 5th in West Germany and another 4th in France. Sadly after this results fell

Above
Gilberto Parlotti (24) push-starts his Tomos during a 1969 international meeting in Italy. Number 7 is a Honda CR110

Above right
The Koper-based Tomos factory as it was in 1969

Right
1971 Tomos GP50 with fibre-glass frame. Note much revised engine from 1969 design. Rider Bernetic and engineer Koccvar are also in photograph

away, but the diminutive Italian still finished an overall 6th in the championship series.

In September 1969 it was announced that the Tomos factory was to market a batch of 50 cc racers for £210 each. The bikes, of which only 12 were to be constructed, would be 'replicas' of the works bikes campaigned that year by Parlotti and Co. The specification included water-cooling, a six-speed gearbox, double-sided drum front brake and 12 bhp at 12,000 rpm. The engine was still based on the familiar Puch-type design.

Parlotti was to give Tomos their best ever GP with

Wind testing the 1979 Tomos GP bike

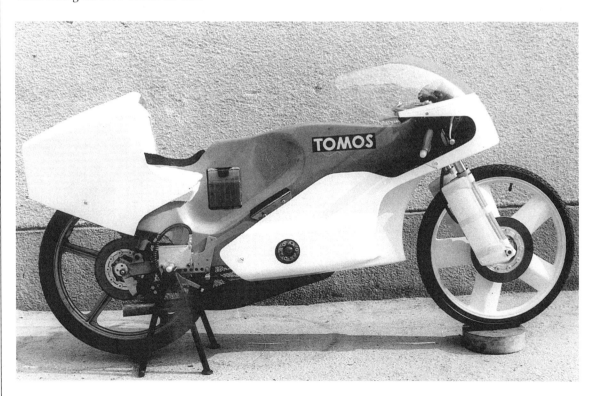

The new 50 cc GP mount which Tomos introduced in 1980. With further development it won the newly *introduced European Championship in 1982, ridden by Zdravko Matulja*

a rostrum position (3rd) in the 1970 West German GP before leaving to ride for the Italian Morbidelli team in the 125 cc class.

He was replaced by another Italian, Luigi Rinaudo who rode the latest Tomos to 4th place in the Czech GP and 7th in the Spanish GP.

That year Tomos had developed a new machine; with a frame of fibre-glass it had a disc valve, water-cooled engine instead of the orthodox piston-port type used in 1969 and 1970. The frame was moulded in two halves which were bonded together. It had a built-in fuel tank, incorporating a transparent strip so that the exact fuel level could be seen at a glance.

Weight of the complete frame was 6.8 kg (15 lb). Of pressed-steel, the rear fork had a narrow pivot so that the rider could tuck his legs in close to reduce the frontal area. The engine had a bore and stroke of 40 x 39.6 mm and revved to 15,500 rpm. Maximum power output was 15.5 bhp. Primary drive was by straight-cut gears to a six-speed close ratio gearbox. Maximum speed was over 100 mph, but it still couldn't match the class-leading Derbi and Kreidler machinery. The next year (1972) Rinaudo was 5th in East Germany, whilst local riders Miklos (6th) and Seljak (9th) upheld Yugoslav honours in the domestic GP at Opatija.

From then on it was downhill all the way, until 1979, when an updated racer was debuted. By now the engine gave around 20 bhp at 17,000 rpm and there were cast alloy wheels, disc brakes front and rear and all-new cosmetics, but the unique fibre-glass chassis was retained. Tomos chose to ignore the championship trail and instead concentrated upon getting the new GP bike right. In the process a completely revised streamlining appeared in 1980, thanks in no small part to the Yugoslav Air Force, which made its wind tunnel facilities available to the Koper bike builders. By the end of 1981 the new bike was ready for action and all this effort was to finally pay off when Zdravko Matulja won the newly introduced European Championship title on his 50 cc Tomos in 1982, following this up with a 4th place in the 1983 Yugoslav GP.

In an article for *Motorcycle Enthusiast* magazine that same year, British journalist Alan Cathcart called Matulja 'Pride of the Tiddlers'. This applied equally to the Tomos effort. Even though their racing was run very much on a shoestring, the Yugoslav company displayed a wealth of mechanical diversity and ingenuity in the smallest capacity racing class, stretching from the early 1960's until the 50 cc class was dropped to make way for the new 80 cc category for the 1984 season. If there was a single word to describe motorcycling in Yugoslavia it would be *Tomos*, supporters of the 50 cc racing class from beginning to end.

Index